AF379462

Christian Valnet

The Big Book of Cocktails

ISBN 978-2-37297-2505

Copyright 2015
Edizioni R.E.I.
www.edizionirei.com
info@edizionirei.com

Index

The Cocktails..9

The glasses Cocktail 15

Alexander 28

Americano 29

Angel face 30

Aviation 31

Bacardi..32

Barracuda...33

Bellini 34

Between the Sheets...35

Black Russian 36

Bloody Mary...37

Bramble 38

B-52 39

Caipirinha 41

Casino 43

Champagne cocktail 44

Clover Club 45

Cosmopolitan 46

Cuba libre...47

Daiquiri 49

Dark'n Stormy 50

Derby 51

Dirty Martini 52

Dry Martini 53

Espresso Martini 54

French Connection 55

French Martini 56

French 75 57

Gin Fizz...58

God Father 60

Golden dream..61

Grasshopper 62

Harvey wallbanger......................................63

Hemingway special......................................64

Horse's Neck 65

Irish coffee 66

Kamikaze 68

Kir 69

Lemon Drop Martini 70

Long Island Iced Tea 71

Mai Tai 73

Manhattan 74

Margarita 75

Mary Pickford 77

Mimosa 78

Mint Julep 79

Mojito 80

Monkey Gland 82

Moscow mule 83

Negroni 84

Old Fashioned 86

Paradise 87

Piña Colada 88

Pisco sour 89

Planter's Punch 90

Porto flip 91

Ramos Fizz 92

Rose 93

Russian Spring Punch 94

Rusty Nail 95

Sazerac 96

Screwdriver 97

Sea breeze 98

Sex on the Beach..99

Sidecar 100

Singapore Sling 101

Spritz..102

Stinger..103

Tequila Sunrise 104

Tom Collins 105

Tommy's Margarita..107

Tuxedo 108

Vampiro 109

Vesper 110

Whisky Sour 111

White lady..112

Yellow bird 113

Other Cocktails 114

Alaska 115

Alpage 116

Andalusia 117

Annalisa 118

Anonimo 119

Bamboo 120

Bentley 121

Blue Lagoon 122

Bronx 123

Bull Shot 124

Cardinale 125

Caruso 126

Claridge 127

Czarina 128

Gibson 129

Gin & French 130

Gin & It 131

Golden Cadillac 132

Grand Slam 133

Jack Rose 134

Japanese Slipper..135

Ladyboy 136

Old Pal 137

Orgasm..138

Rob Roy 139

White Russian 140

The Cocktails

A cocktail is a drink obtained by a proportionate and balanced mixture of different alcoholic ingredients, no alcohol and aromas. A well-executed cocktails must have structure, flavor and color balanced; if performed without the use of alcohol component is called non-alcoholic cocktails.

The cocktail may present inside the cup of the ice, not present at all (as some cocktails winter such as grog), or it can be only cooled with ice. A particular class of cocktails is constituted by the shot, small cocktail that may have all the characteristics of a normal and cocktails are served in two types of glasses, the shot and bite. To prevent the abuse of both fictitious names of cocktails is unauthorized modifications to cocktails known, the International Bartenders Association (IBA) has codified 60 to which each year are added or eliminated other cocktails.

The International Bartenders Association, founded on Feb. 24, 1951 in the Saloon of the Grand Hotel in Torquay, United Kingdom, is an organization of barman. The organization is also in charge of drawing up the list of IBA Official Cocktail.

November 25, 2011 was the official new list of cocktails IBA which at the moment are 77, divided into three categories:
1. Contemporary Classics.
2. The Unforgettables.
3. New Era Drinks.

Contemporary Classics (31 cocktails):

- Bellini
- Black Russian
- Bloody Mary
- Caipirinha
- Champagne Cocktail
- Cosmopolitan
- Cuba libre
- French Connection
- God Father
- God Mother

- Golden dream
- Grasshopper
- French 75
- Harvey wallbanger
- Hemingway special
- Horse's Neck
- Irish coffee
- Kir
- Long Island Iced Tea
- Mai Tai
- Margarita
- Mimosa
- Mojito
- Moscow mule
- Mint Julep
- Piña Colada
- Rose
- Sea Breeze
- Sex on the Beach
- Singapore Sling
- Tequila Sunrise

The Unforgettables (30 cocktails):

- Alexander
- Americano
- Angel Face
- Aviation
- Bacardi
- Between the Sheets
- Casino
- Clover Club
- Daiquiri
- Derby
- Dry Martini
- Gin Fizz
- John Collins

- Manhattan
- Mary Pickford
- Monkey Gland
- Negroni
- Old Fashioned
- Paradise
- Planter's Punch
- Porto flip
- Ramos Fizz
- Rusty Nail
- Sazerac
- Screwdriver
- Sidecar
- Stinger
- Tuxedo
- Whiskey Sour
- White lady

New Era Drinks (16 cocktails):

- Barracuda
- Bramble
- B-52
- Dark 'n' Stormy
- Dirty Martini
- Espresso Martini
- French Martini
- Kamikaze
- Lemon Drop Martini
- Pisco sour
- Russian Spring Punch
- Spritz Veneziano
- Tommy's Margarita
- Vampiro
- Vesper
- Yellow Bird

The factors characterizing the classification are:
* Structure
* Capacity
* Service temperature
* Moment of consumption

The result is the following classification that appears to be the most used and is divided into:

* **Pre dinner** - are served as aperitifs, from Latin aperire (open); many are characterized by the property to stimulate salivation and, consequently, the appetite.
  The main features that contain the mix drinks can be slightly bittering, dried or bite, slightly citrigne, delicately fruity and floral. Sparkling wines, mixed with other products with the aperitif is a great prelude to the meal. In Italy they are often supported by snacks contour.

* **After dinner** - Served after dinner, but not to be confused with the digestive, can be digestive or replace and \ or to accompany a dessert.
  In this category we are used which tend distilled aged brandy, cognac, rum, whiskey, but you can also use vodka, tequila and brandy.
  Flavorings consist of sweet liqueurs, bitters, bitters, vermouth and dyes, may be the same or even colored liqueurs syrups. They are also used for fruit juices (orange, lemon, pineapple, tropical), coffee, cream, eggs. The after dinner cocktail classics with a good structure is used in almost every cup cocktail, if you add juice, cream, coffee can serve double cocktail glass; if the cocktail provides the ice serves in a tumbler, the cocktails with sparkling wine or champagne are served in flutes.

  They are characterized by:
  1. Presence of strong alcohol.
  2. Presence of liqueurs and creams.

3. Presence of taste and smell complex.

- **Long drinks** - The long drinks are alcoholic and soft drinks, whose volume varies between 25 cl and 30 cl.
  They are refreshing and thirst-quenching drink that you drink at any time and hence the long drink alcohol it should be in moderation (the alcohol content should be maintained at around 20% of the volume).
  Whether alcohol is non-alcoholic, refreshing and are generally characterized by:
  1. Presence of large variety of spirits and liqueurs.
  2. Use of important fruit juices and carbonated drinks, juices and vegetable centrifuges.
  3. Presence of massive and very colorful decorations.

- **Any time** - are the ones that can be drunk at any time and at any time of the day and are characterized by:
  1. Presence of alcohol-based.
  2. Adding soft drinks.
  3. Using softeners (or glucose under saccarosi).

The classification is needed to ensure the realization of cocktails according to specific rules, regardless of the location and the operator who applies it, preserving the organoleptic characteristics and dosing.
The types of cocktails that we find are:
- Short, if served in a cocktail glass.
- Medium if served in tumblers or old fashioned.
- Long drinks if served in tall tumbler glasses or other high-capacity.

Three are the phases of preparation of a cocktail:

1. **The base** - The base is the element around which is the cocktail, usually it is a white spirit that gives structure to the drink.
    For neutral structure is used:
    - Vodka.
    - Rum light.

- Rum industry.

For a structure particularly characterized using:

- Bourbon Whiskey.
- Scotch whiskey.
- Cachaca.
- Rum agriculture.

For a structure strongly characterized using:

- Gin
- Tequila
- Aged rums

2. **The dye** - Dye is the element that enriches the range odor and taste; liqueurs and creams are generally used ones that give fragrance and taste. The dyes do not really color the cocktail, but the spice. The colorants can be divided, according to their sugar content, in two categories:

Sugar content 180 g / l:

- Vermouth
- Cointreau
- Benedictine
- Galliano

Sugar content 220 g / l:

- Baileys
- Rum Cream
- Tia Maria
- Lemon cream

3. **The flavoring** - The flavor improves the color and the pleasantness of the drink, is a soft drink like cola, tonic, syrups, fruit. In cocktail influences the visual appearance and taste.

The glasses Cocktail

The type of glass is very important to serve a cocktail.
There are various types that change of form and dimensions.
Each cocktail must be served in a particular glass, able to enhance the features: for many drinks, especially for seventy-seven international cocktails encoded by IBA, in the recipe itself is indicated as the glass will have to be of service.
The choice of glass is correct index of aesthetic sense and attention to detail; It is very important to pay attention not to touch the edge of the glasses with your fingers: you should always lift them by keeping them from the stem, or from the bottom.
Below we present an overview of the main cocktail glasses, although it will hardly be possible to obtain them all: the fundamental ones are the cocktail glass, the tumbler, the highball and flutes.

Cocktail glass "Martini"

It is the classic martini cocktail glass, triangular and long-stemmed.
It has a capacity of about 100 ml and is used in particular for short drink alcohol served without ice: the wide surface of this glass is, in fact, able to put in evidence the aromas and the color that characterize the drink. The shank allows the sealing of the glass without affecting the temperature of the beverage.

Double cocktail glass "Martini"

This glass has a shape identical to the cocktail glass, but a size and a capacity superior: it is, in fact, able to contain a dose almost the double of liquid (about 200 ml). It is used for cocktails without ice, made with ingredients not excessively alcoholic (such as juices or wines).

Cup Champagne

The traditional champagne glass, in addition to the classic Champagne cocktail can be used as a dark glass to serve drinks and sparkling. It is also suitable to drink made from citrus juices spirits such as Daiquiri, Bacardi and other cocktails belonging to the category of sour.

Goblet or chalice great

Chalice given to drink with crushed ice or fragmented as the Sherry Cobbler and for crusta or cocktails where the glass is rimmed with sugar. Also called copita or tulip, is a glass rod shaped slightly paunchy that closes towards the opening.

Balloon

This glass has become the quintessential glass of cognac and
large brandy.
The large surface area helps to evaporate the aroma of brandy,
while the narrow opening helps to trap the flavor of the drink in
the glass. The glass can usually hold between 180-240 ml, but to
enjoy the best product you should pay only 60-90 ml each time.
They grab the cup resting on the palm of the hand; This helps to
warm up a little liqueur and then also in the aroma sprigionarne
To avoid heat it before serving any kind of cognac or brandy
lose so all its strengths.

Tumbler

"Old fashioned", "Rocks glass", or "Lowball" is a glass bottom for liquor on the rocks with ice or cocktails with few ingredients. Cylindrical glass, low and wide, with a capacity of approximately 180 ml. Thanks to its ability to contain a fair amount of cubes, is used to serve liquor on-the-rock and short drinks that require the presence of ice (such as, for example, the Negroni).
Almost always the cocktail is mixed directly into the glass.

List of cocktails to be served in the glass Tumbler:
- Ada Cocktail
- Apple Sour II
- Armagnac Sour
- B and B
- Big Boy
- Black Russian II
- Brandy and soda
- Brandy Buck
- Campari Negroni
- Chicago Cooler

- Cognac Amer
- Cognac Sour
- Crash Virgin Colada
- Frutta Caramellata
- Gin Old Fashioned
- Jam
- Maximilian
- Minimi
- Pepper Tonic
- Piccante
- Rusty Nail
- Tequila Sour

Lowball or Collins

It serves for cocktails medium long, as the mojito or caipirinha, which contain ice, or for cocktails such as the American, where it is added to the soda, as the "Whisky and soda", or to fruit juice, tomato juice and fruit.
The usable volume is about 30 cl.

Highball

It is ideal for drinks and long drinks, for double whiskey and mineral waters. Still higher than the previous glass, it is able to contain about 350 ml of liquid. It is the ideal glass for serving long drinks (especially those little alcohol, served with ice in summer). It is also called Delmonico, the name of who first launched the fashion.

Glass for Irish coffee

It is a goblet slightly domed, the capacity of about 180 ml, indicated to serve Irish Coffee and other hot drinks (such as punch and grog): the stem allows, in fact, a secure grip without there being burned fingers.

List of cocktails to be served in the glass Irish coffee:
- Choc Grand Marnier
- Irish Coffee

Flute

It is a classic glass where are served the sparkling (a category of light cocktails made with sparkling wine and fresh fruit, such as Bellini, Puccini and Mimosa) and sparkling wines or champagne buckets in general (who need to free up slowly 'carbon dioxide). It has a slender, with short stem and thin, a cup very narrow and elongated, unable to retain aromas and bubbles.

List of cocktails to be served in Flute:
- Bellini
- Brandy Crusta
- Brandy Daisy
- Buck's Fizz
- Champ
- Champagne cocktail
- Cognac Framboise

- Cognac Orange
- Creamy Orange
- Hemingway's Rum cocktail
- James Bond
- Kir
- Kir Royal
- Kiwi Kir Royal
- Mimosa
- Number One
- Pomme d'Amour
- Punch Al Brandy e Champagne
- Rossini
- Something Sassy

Alexander

• Category: The Unforgettables.
• Glass: cocktail glass.

The Alexander is an after dinner cocktail made with brandy, cream with cocoa brown and cream. It was created in London in 1922 by Henry Mc Elhone with the name "Panama".

Recipe:
> • 3 cl cognac
> • 3 cl cocoa cream dark
> • 3 cl cream.

Shake in a shaker with ice, strain and serve in a cocktail glass. Garnish with grated (or sprinkling) of nutmeg.
It seems that the first name of this cocktail was Panama, where it was used instead of Cognac Gin, from which the variant Gin Alexandra.
> • 1/3 gin
> • 1/3 of cocoa cream white
> • 1/3 creamy.

Shake all ingredients (except nutmeg) with ice in a shaker, then sprinkle with nutmeg and serve over.

Americano

• Category: The Unforgettables.
• Glass: Old Fashion.

The American is an Italian pre dinner cocktails which, despite its name, uses only Italian products: bitter Campari, red vermouth and soda.
The American is prepared with the technical build (building directly in the glass) and is served in a glass Old Fashion.

Recipe:
> • 3 cl Campari
> • 3 cl Red Vermouth
> • A splash of soda.

Then pours into the glass filled with ice Red Vermouth and Bitter, then you go with Soda water which is slightly mixed using the stirrer or simple straw.
Eventually it squeezes and gets inside a cocktail lemon zest and a slice of orange as decoration.

Angel face

• Category: The Unforgettables.
• Glass: cocktail glass.

Angel Face is an all-day cocktail made with gin, apricot brandy and calvados, of French origin.

Recipe:
> • 3 cl gin
> • 3 cl apricot brandy
> • 3 cl calvados.

Take a cocktail glass and fill it with ice.
Add in a shaker 3 cl gin, apricot brandy and 3 cl 3 cl calvados and stir.
Remove ice from the cup and pour the contents of the shaker. Serve without straw.

Aviation

• Category: The Unforgettables.
• Glass: cocktail glass.

The Aviation is an all day cocktail made with gin and maraschino created in 1916, during the First World War, in honor of the British pilots. This drink has two possible creators:

- The first tells of the improvisation of a barman in a circle of Air Force officers who mixed it in honor of the British pilots (WWI). It was often used as a commemorative cocktail or a ritual, in which pilots toasted their return.
- The second theory equates the creator as the first to write down the recipe, Hugo Ensslin, in 1916, dedicating it to the pioneers of aviation.

Recipe:
- 4.5 cl gin
- 1.5 cl maraschino
- 1.5 cl of creme de violette - optional
- 1.5 cl fresh lemon juice
- Lemon zest or a maraschino cherry.

It is prepared in a cocktail glass cooled with ice. In a shaker they are paid 4.5 cl of gin, 1.5 cl of maraschino, 1.5 cl of creme de violette (optional) and 1.5 cl fresh lemon juice, all mixed and poured into a cocktail glass previously emptied the ice.
The cocktail is garnished with a maraschino cherry (or a maraschino cherry) or with lemon peel spiral.

Bacardi

• Category: The Unforgettables.
• Glass: cocktail glass.

Bacardi is a pre-dinner cocktail, a variation of Daiquiri (which contains rum, lime juice or lemon juice and sugar syrup, instead of grenadine syrup).
The version that we know today was born in the US and the first recipes appeared to 1917.

Recipe:
  • 4.5 cl of rum Bacardi white
  • 2 cl lemon juice
  • 1.5 cl grenadine syrup.

Shake all ingredients and strain into a chilled cocktail.
The distillate Bacardi is related to Don Facundo Bacardi. Born in Catalonia, then he moved to Santiago de Cuba to start a trade in wines. Then in 1862 he bought a still and began the distillation of molasses from sugar cane plantations nearby.
His ron (rum) which spread first in Havana and then in Florida, was a great success.
In 1960 Fidel Castro, with a coup, he nationalized the distilleries of Santiago, but the company had had time to move to Mexico and Puerto Rico. Bacardi is today one of the largest producers of alcohol in the world and has distilleries in the Bahamas, Brazil, Canada, Venezuela and Martinique, for a total of over 200 million bottles produced.

Barracuda

• Category: Drinks New Era.
• Glass: lowball.

It is a very nice cocktail, pleasantly tangy, very appealing. It can be an excellent aperitif or a drink to be enjoyed on several occasions of the day.

Recipe:
  • 4.5 cl Rum Gold
  • 1.5 cl Galliano
  • 6 cl Pineapple Juice
  • 1 cl fresh lime juice
  • 1 cl sugar syrup
  • Top with Champagne or Prosecco.

Having shaken the ingredients quickly with the crystalline ice, pour, filtering the mixture into a lowball filled with ice.
Complete with chilled champagne, decorating the glass with straws, the slice of lemon and a maraschino cherry.

Bellini

• Category: Contemporary Classics.
• Glass: flute.

The Bellini is a cocktail pre dinner belonging to the category of long drinks made with sparkling white wine, usually sparkling, and pulp and pureed white peach juice.
It is one of the most internationally known Italian cocktails.

Recipe:
      • 10 cl of Prosecco
      • 5 cl of peach pulp.

The original recipe wants the use of pulp and white peach juice Verona, crushed and blended, mixed with sparkling wine slowly so as not to cause excessive loss of gas; serve in a flute.
Because of the difficult traceability of white peaches and Prosecco in some areas of the world, there are many variations. If we use the Champagne, it becomes a Royal Bellini. Some, however, argue that the champagne is not the best paired with the delicate flavor of white peach Bellini.
Other variants are the Rossini with strawberries instead of fishing, the Mimosa with fresh orange juice and Tintoretto typical of neighboring areas of Venice with pomegranate juice.
The Bellini was invented in 1948 by Giuseppe Cipriani, head bartender at Harry's Bar. Due to its pink color that reminded Cipriani color of the toga of a saint in a painting by Giovanni Bellini, he appointed the Bellini cocktail.

Between the Sheets

• Category: The Unforgettables.
• Glass: cocktail cup.

For some sources, the "Between the Sheets" he was created by the hand of the great Harry MacElhone bartender at Harry's New York Bar in Paris in 1930; character that accredits the creation of the "Sidecar". According to other sources, the drink was created by the former director, Mr. Polly Berkeley Hotel in London in 1921.

Recipe:
  • 4/10 Brandy
  • 3/10 White rum
  • 1/10 Cointreau or Triple sec
  • 2/10 Lemon juice.

Put brandy, white rum, triple sec and lemon juice in a shaker with crushed ice.
Shekerare vigorously, then filtered into cocktail glass cup.
The original version of this cocktail (3/10 Brandy 3/10 White rum, Cointreau 3/10, a teaspoon of lemon juice) is, according to some, liqueur and heavy enough.

Black Russian

• Category: Contemporary Classics.
• Glass: highball small.

The Black Russian is a cocktail after dinner born in 1949 from the creativity of Gustave Tops, barman at the Hotel Metropole in Brussels. The cocktail was prepared for the US ambassador to Luxembourg Pearl Mesta.
A variant of the Black Russian is the White Russian.

Recipe:
> • 5 cl of vodka
> • 2 cl coffee liqueur (Kahlua usually).

Pour vodka and coffee liqueur directly in small tumbler with ice and garnish with the lemon zest.

Bloody Mary

• Category: Contemporary Classics.
• Glass: highball.

The Bloody Mary is a pre-dinner cocktail made with vodka, tomato juice and hot spices or flavorings such as Worcestershire sauce, Tabasco, horseradish, celery, salt, black pepper, cayenne pepper and the juice lemon.

Recipe:
  • 4.5 cl of vodka
  • 9 cl of tomato juice
  • 1.5 cl lemon juice
  • 2/3 drops of Worcester sauce
  • 1 pinch of salt and black pepper
  • Tabasco.

Can be vigorously shaken or stirred slowly in the tumbler, the result will be the same.
The Bloody Mary was almost certainly created by George Jessel around 1939. The epithet "Bloody Mary" is associated with several female characters, historical or fictional, especially Queen Mary I of England.
It is believed that the inspiration for the cocktail was the Hollywood star Mary Pickford, who previously had a similar cocktail consisting of rum, grenadine and maraschino bearing his name.

Bramble

• Category: Drinks New Era.
• Glass: tumbler.

The Bramble is one of the cocktails that gave birth to the category of "New Era Drinks" cocktails encoded IBA. Its origin dates back to 1986 in the Soho district of London, specifically in "Fred's club".

Recipe:
• 4.5 cl Gin
• 1.5 cl lemon juice
• 1.5 cl Liqueur More
• 1 cl sugar syrup.

The Bramble is prepared with the technical Build.
Take into a tumbler with ice and pour gin, lemon juice and sugar syrup with the help of a Bar Spoon, mix thoroughly pouring last (in a circular fashion), the blackberry liqueur.
Bramble garnish with a slice of lemon and two blackberries.

B-52

• Category: Drinks New Era.
• Glass: .In Italy is usually served in a cocktail glass, the rest of Europe and the USA It is served in the glass "shot".

The B-52 is an after dinner cocktail was born in the United States consists primarily of Kahlua, Baileys and Grand Marnier cream.
Its preparation involves a technique in layers, whereby due to the different densities of the ingredients, they tend to remain separate instead of mixing. It is served in a chilled Martini, and has many variations, such as shot, or inflamed even if it is not accepted as a professional construction.
Cocktail of this kind, with horizontal division, are defined layers, also their preparation is said construction, since it is opposite to the shake or stir.

Recipe:
- 1 part coffee liqueur (Tia Maria or Kahlua)
- 1 part cream Baileys
- 1 part Grand Marnier.

First is poured in the glass the coffee liqueur (eg Tia Maria or Kahlua), then pour the cream Baileys very slowly by sliding the back of a cocktail spoon, those with very long handle, taking care to disturb as little as possible the lower layer by pouring the upper one. Similarly, again with much attention, pouring the Grand Marnier over the whole.
For a more choreographic be drunk inflamed: just set fire to the Grand Marnier with a lighter and within seconds will catch fire.

Variants:
  • B-52 with Bombay Doors, a B-52 with Bombay gin
  • B-52 in the desert, a B-52 with tequila instead of Baileys
  • B-52, a B-52 with Cointreau
  • B-53, a B-52 with Vodka
  • B-54, a B-52 with Amaretto
  • B-55, a B-52 with Absinthe
  • B-57, a B-52 with Sambuca and Baileys instead of triple sec instead of Grand Marnier.

The name refers to the long-range bomber Boeing B-52 Stratofortress, which was used in the Vietnam War to drop bombs incendiary napalm (and it's probably what did the version flammable).

Caipirinha

• Category: Contemporary Classics.
• Glass: highball or old fashioned.

The caipirinha is a Brazilian cocktail any time typically, made with cachaça, lime, sugar and ice white.
Brazil is served in most restaurants and is considered one drink characteristic of the country.

Recipe:
- 6 cl of cachaça
- half a lime
- sugar cane processed white (3 teaspoons)
- ground ice.

Preparation Tools:
- pestle (useful for the processing of ingredients)
- glass type highball or old fashioned (necessary to contain the pieces of lime)
- 2 short straws.

Preparation of cocktails:
- Cut the lime in half and then in all 4 pieces of equal size; place them in the glass old fashion.
- Add sugar and pestle press lightly on the pulp of the lime; it is useful to perform rotational movements to release the juice, taking care not to squeeze too bitter peel
- adding the ice cubes cleaved and finally the cachaça
- as a garnish to add a slice of lime (thinly sliced) by inserting the edge of the glass
- serve the drink with two straws.

The drink should not be shaken or stirred, but is mixed with the stirrer.

Possibly you should pass the lime juice on the edge of the glass, then add brown sugar: this leaves a layer sweetened leaving more flavor and taste the Caipirinha.

There are many cocktail resulting from Caipirinha, wherein the cachaça is replaced with other spirits:

- The Caipiroska, where vodka replaces cachaça.
- The Caipiroska Negra (also known as Black Caipiroshka or Caipiblack) made with black vodka.
- The Caipirão, made with liquor Portuguese Beirão instead of cachaça.

Casino

• Category: The Unforgettables.
• Glass: cocktail glass.

The Casino is an all day cocktail made of gin, maraschino and orange bitters.

Recipe:
  • 4 cl of dry gin (Old Tom Gin)
  • 1 cl maraschino
  • 1 cl orange bitters
  • 1 cl fresh lemon juice
  • 1 maraschino cherry.

Take a cocktail glass and fill it with ice. In a second glass, add 4 cl of Old Tom Gin, 1 cl maraschino, 1 cl orange bitters and 1 cl fresh lemon juice, then pour into a cocktail shaker filled with ice and shake.
Pour into a cocktail glass from which you removed the ice. Garnish with a maraschino cherry.
Serve without straw.

Champagne cocktail

• Category: Contemporary Classics.
• Glass: flute.

The champagne cocktail is a cocktail pre dinner and was born in the '30s, it seems, from a competition between journalists, whose winner was such Dougherty.

Recipe:
> • 9 cl champagne or sparkling wine
> • 1 cl brandy.

It is prepared directly in a flute, recline down a sugar cube with two drops of Angostura bitters, then brandy and champagne. Garnish with an orange slice and a maraschino cherry.

Clover Club

• Category: The Unforgettables.
• Glass: cocktail glass.

The Clover Club is an all day cocktail made with gin and raspberry syrup.

Recipe:
  • 4.5 cl gin
  • 1.5 cl of raspberry syrup
  • 1.5 cl fresh lemon juice
  • Drops of egg white.

Pour into a shaker filled with ice previously 4.5 cl Gin, 1.5 cl of raspberry juice and 1.5 cl fresh lemon juice. Complete by adding a few drops to a half egg white.
Stir everything well. Strain the contents into a cocktail glass. Serve without straw.

Cosmopolitan

• Category: Contemporary Classics.
• Glass: double cocktail glass.

The Cosmopolitan is a cocktail any time based on vodka.

Recipe:
  • 4.0 cl of Vodka
  • 1.5 cl of Cointreau
  • 1.5 cl of lime juice
  • 3.0 cl of cranberry juice (cranberry).

Shake with ice and serve abundant in double cocktail glass previously cooled.
Garnish with a slice of lime.
Replacing the liqueur Cointreau complementary with blue curacao you get the "Purple Rain", a Cosmopolitan purple very effective.

Cuba libre

• Category: Contemporary Classics.
• Glass: highball.

The Cuba libre is a cocktail any time belonging to the category of long drinks made with white rum and cola. Similar to rum & cola, the two terms I am often used interchangeably, although indicating two different cocktails.

Recipe:
    • 5 cl light rum
    • 12 cl Cola
    • 1 cl lime juice.

Serve in a high ball glass with ice, garnish with a slice of lime.
The origin of the cocktail is rather uncertain.
The hypothesis most commonly credited states that the Cuba Libre was born between 1900 and 1902 in Havana, during the Spanish-American War and the conquest of Cuba's independence from Spain with the help of the United States. The Cuban and US soldiers used to mix cola, imported to Cuba for the first time in those years, with rum.
Various assumptions on the name of the inventor: some sources date the recipe to a soldier, named after covering John Doe, who ordered the American Bar Calle Neptune, a bar by two Americans in the Cuban capital, "Coca Cola American, Cuban rum into a glass filled with ice and a splash of lime ", after toasting" to free Cuba ", the battle cry of the guerrillas.
According to a deposition of 1965 Fausto Rodriguez, a messenger of the Cuban army, the soldier would be Captain Russell of the bodies of American communication.
Another theory suggests that it was a Cuban bartender to mix Coca Cola (typical product US) rum (typical Cuban product) to symbolically unite the two nations.
Some believe barman appreciable adding 1 or 2 drops of angostura before mixing; but if you add or replace one of the two

original components other ingredients are obtained these variants:

• Cuba libre pounded, with the addition of half a lime cut into four parts and a spoonful of brown sugar. In the preparation of Cuba libre pounded the addition of cane sugar and the need to integrate it with the other ingredients with a mixing more marked it helps to decrease the effervescence and to modify the sweetness of the cocktail, which is why some believe the barman preparing a non-optimal .

- Rum & Coke, also known as rum and coke, involves the use of cola and rum, eliminating files
- Cuba libre Cuban, with 3-4 ounces of amber rum and the addition of sweet'n'sour.
- Cubotto, prepared by replacing the cola the bitter orange.
- Cubanta, prepared by replacing the cola Fanta.
- Cobra, prepared by replacing the rum Braulio.
- bull Cuba, replacing the Red Bull cola.

To note the change more consistent, which led to the birth of a whole new cocktail, the Santo Libre, a rum and Sprite - gaseous.

It owes its name to the island of Santo Domingo where it was invented and where, of course, it is famous ..

The need to call the cocktails in a different manner is caused by a clear indication of the origin of Cuba libre and so it was necessary to emphasize the different place of origin.

The Santo Libre is much less known of the "big brother" but is slowly spreading thanks to all the people, visiting the Dominican Republic, discover it and appreciate it.

The recipe calls for:
- • 4/10 rum Blanco
- • 6/10 Gassosa
- • Limon (lime).

Serve in highball glass filled with ice after mixing gently without shaker. The only variation is the use of amber rum in place of the white.

Daiquiri

• Category: The Unforgettables.
• Glass: cocktail glass.

The Daiquiri cocktails any time of Caribbean origins made from white rum, lime juice and sugar syrup.
It served primarily in a cocktail glass, the glass changes only in case takes fruity variations. There are many variations, but the only accepted between IBA cocktails are the Frozen Daiquiri and the Banana Daiquiri.

Recipe:
    • 4.5 cl of white rum
    • 2 cl fresh lemon juice
    • 0.5 cl of sugar syrup

Prepare in a shaker and strain into a cocktail glass undecorated.
A variant is the Superior Daiquiri cocktail that has its origins in Puerto Rico in 1962, recipe rediscovered in 2012 in Italy in an old manual dell'UKBG; The recipe calls for the use of tangerine juice to replace the lime and a drop of bitter Campari making it very Italian.

Dark'n Stormy

• Category: Drinks New Era.
• Glass: highball.

Dark'n Stormy is a cocktail Long drink beverage became a symbol of Bermuda, where took his birth.
Do you know the name of its creator, but his reputation is unparalleled. That's Dark'n Stormy is one of the mixtures are easier to prepare, created by the simple combination of dark rum and ginger beer; the Dark'n Stormy, spread very quickly in Australia.

Recipe:
> • 6 cl dark rum
> • 10 cl Ginger Beer, soda drink made with ginger.

Pour the rum into a glass filled high ball previously for ice, then add the ginger ale.
Decorate the glass with a slice of lime.

Derby

• Category: The Unforgettables.
• Glass: cocktail glass.

The Derby is an all day cocktail made with gin, peach bitters and mint.

Recipe:
- 6 cl gin
- 2 drops of peach bitters
- 2 mint leaves.

Fill a cocktail glass with ice and a mixing glass. Add in the mixing glass 6 cl gin and 2 drops of peach bitters, then mix well. Filter the contents of the mixing glass in a cocktail glass after removing the ice in it.
Garnish with two mint leaves.
Serve without straw.

Dirty Martini

• Category: Drinks New Era.
• Glass: Martini Cup.

The Dirty Martini is a pre-dinner cocktail classic, close relative of the true Martini.
Unlike the original, which is made with gin, the Dirty Martini is made with vodka and is 'dirty' with the brine in which the olives are kept.

Recipe:
> • 75 ml of Vodka
> • 15 ml of dry vermouth
> • 15 ml of brine of olives
> • Decoration: olive.

1. Fill a shaker up to ¾ of its capacity with ice.
2. Pour into the shaker the precise amount of vodka, dry vermouth and brine.
3. Using a cocktail spoon, mix the ingredients thoroughly, for about 5-10 seconds. Do not mix too hard to avoid shake too ingredients or to break the ice cubes.
4. Using a strainer barman (strainer), strain the cocktail into the glass service (martini glass) and decorate it with an olive.

Dry Martini

• Category: The Unforgettables.
• Glass: Martini Cup.

The Dry Martini is a famous pre-dinner cocktails made with gin and dry vermouth.

Recipe:
- 6 cl gin
- 1 cl dry vermouth
- 1 olive green
- 1 slice of lemon.

1. Take a cup from Martini and fill it with ice cubes so as to simultaneously cooling the walls and keep her very cold throughout the preparation of cocktails, then also fill a mixing glass with ice cubes.
2. Eliminate excess water from mixing glass. Flavor ice adding 1 cl dry vermouth into a mixing glass, stirring well. Remove the ice cubes from the martini cup once brought to room temperature.
3. Pour the vermouth in a martini glass filtering it from the ice.
4. Repeat the flavoring of ice remained in the mixing glass, this time with 6 cl gin.
5. Pour the gin in a martini glass, always filtering it from the ice. Lightly squeeze the oil to a piece of lemon zest over the cocktail.
6. Add as seal olive green.

Espresso Martini

• Category: Drinks New Era.
• Glass: cocktail glass.

The Espresso Martini is a cocktail atypical, very particular, which lends itself well to be drunk after dinner, especially if accompanied with cakes, chocolate cakes, chocolate cheesecake and trifle.

Recipe:
> • 5 cl Vodka
> • 5 cl Sugar syrup
> • 1 cl Kahlua, coffee liqueur
> • 1 short espresso.

Pour all ingredients in a shaker with ice.
Shake. Filtered cup cold cocktail.
Basically it's a blended coffee reinforced by alcohol, not much different as a concept from the classic coffee laced with grappa.
The original recipe calls for only vodka, but it can be proven with an excellent grappa, for a cocktail at the coffee even more nuanced and intriguing.

French Connection

• Category: Contemporary Classics.
• Glass: tumbler.

Born in the United States in the late '50s, the French Connection is a sophisticated cocktail after dinner sweet taste and red color amber; composed in equal parts of Cognac and Amaretto.

Recipe:
    • 3.5 cl of cognac
    • 3.5 cl amaretto

The preparation of cocktails French Connection takes place directly in the Old Fashioned glass.
First you need to add a few ice cubes in the glass, after this we must add the Cognac and Amaretto in equal parts. Before serving should be mixed it very gently, so that the ingredients blend well.
Finally serve the French Connection without any decoration.

French Martini

• Category: Drinks New Era.
• Glass: cocktail glass.

At first glance there seems to be little French in this pre-dinner cocktail, in fact the key ingredient is the raspberry liqueur. Among the various brands, we mention the Chambord, which produces a raspberry liqueur blacks, with honey, vanilla and some herbs.
Chambord is produced in France for over 300 years (from 1685) and is a sweet liqueur and tasty.

Recipe:
  • 4.5 cl Vodka
  • 1.5 cl Chambord raspberry liqueur
  • 1.5 cl Fresh pineapple juice.

Pour all ingredients in a mixing glass with ice cubes. Mix well. Strain into chilled cocktail glass. Twist of lemon.

French 75

• Category: Contemporary Classics.
• Glass: flute.

The French 75 is a cocktail made with gin, champagne and lemon juice, created for the first time by one of the Barman who made the history of cocktails, Harry Macelhone, owner in 1915 of Harry's American Bar in Paris.
This particular Long Drink, takes its name from the French guns used during World War I, just called French 75. Although legend has it his birth on French territory today its creation has been attributed to the United States; origins aside, the French 75 is one of the classic cocktails ideal as an aperitif.

Recipe:
  • 6 cl of champagne
  • 3 cl gin
  • 1.5 cl lemon juice
  • 2 drops of sugar syrup

In a shaker pour 3 cl Gin, 1.5 cl lemon juice and two drops of sugar syrup. Shake and strain into a flute. Complete adding 6 cl of champagne.
Mix gently.
An old recipe replaces the Gin with Cognac to attribute the birth of the French 75 France.

Gin Fizz

• Category: The Unforgettables.
• Glass: highball.

Gin Fizz is a cocktail any time, a long drink made of gin and soda. Alcohol is generally 15%.

Recipe:
- 4.5 cl gin
- 3 cl fresh lemon juice
- 1 cl sugar syrup
- 8 cl of soda.

Take a highball glass type and fill it with ice cubes. Take a shaker and fill it in turn to ice cubes. Add in a cup of simple syrup 1 cl, 4.5 cl gin and 3 cl fresh lemon juice.
Remove excess water from the shaker, pour the ingredients and shake. Dall'highball remove ice and pour the solution obtained.
Complete adding 8 cl of soda. Garnish with lemon zest to store within the High ball and a slice of lemon on the glass. Serve without straw.

A variant is the Ramos Gin Fizz.
Recipe:
- 4.5 cl gin
- 1.5 cl fresh lemon juice
- 1.5 cl fresh lime juice
- 3 cl simple syrup
- 6 cl of cream (heavy cream)
- 3 drops of orange flower water
- 2 drops of vanilla extract
- 1 egg white
- soda

- Take a collins, add 4.5 cl Gin 1.5 cl fresh lemon juice 1.5 cl fresh lime juice and simple syrup 3 cl.

- Then, add three drops of orange flower water, then a few drops of vanilla extract.
- Add 6 cl of cream (heavy cream) and the white of an egg. Put everything in a shaker without ice and shake for 3 minutes, then repeat the operation by filling it with ice. In theory it should agitate for a total of 12 minutes.
- Pour into collins glass without ice.
- Then add soda to the brim of the glass. Serve with a straw.

God Father

• Category: Contemporary Classics.
• Glass: tumbler.

Godfather is an after dinner cocktail made with Scotch and Amaretto which is prepared directly in the old fashion tumbler with ice.

Recipe:
   • 4.5 cl Scotch
   • 2.5 cl Amaretto di Saronno.

There is also the variant with vodka instead of scotch, named Mother of God. The proportions remain unchanged.

Golden dream

• Category: Contemporary Classics.
• Glass: cocktail glass.

The Golden Dream is a cocktail after dinner that comes all the way from Florida sixties. It seems that its creator was Raimundo Alvarez barman of 'Old King Bar in Miami, who created this cocktail in honor of the famous actress Joan Crawford.

Recipe:
• 2.0 cl of liqueur Galliano (sweetened hydro-alcoholic infusion of various herbs and spices such as anise, licorice and vanilla)
• 2.0 cl of Cointreau
• 2.0 cl of juice d 'orange
• 2.0 cl of liquid cream.

Introduce all the ingredients in a shaker with ice. Shake vigorously for a few seconds and strain into a cocktail glass type. The Golden Dream is a variation of the Golden Cadillac cocktail, the difference is that in the Golden Dream is not present the Creme de Cacao which was replaced by the Cointreau. Golden Dream, literally "golden dream", is a cocktail that already just by its name tells us that it is a drink to be consumed as a digestive after a hearty dinner.
Its preparation is among the most popular especially in Japan and Canada.

Grasshopper

• Category: Contemporary Classics.
• Glass: cocktail glass.

The Grasshopper is an after dinner cocktail creamy and pale green, reminiscent of that of a grasshopper (in English "grasshopper"). A variation of less alcohol better known "Alexander" made with gin, creme de cacao and cream.
It has been realized for the first time in the US in the 50s. It's a cool cocktail and delicate ideal for after dinner in the summer, and at all times for those who love the creams and delicate flavors.

Recipe:
  • 3.0 cl of cream mint green
  • 3.0 cl of crème de cacao white
  • 3.0 cl of cream.

Pour all ingredients into a cocktail shaker filled with ice. Shake vigorously for several seconds and serve in a well chilled cocktail glass.
There are several variants of this cocktail.
For example the "vodka grasshopper" to do just replace the cream with vodka in equal amounts, or the "brown grasshopper", which replaces the cream of mint green with cocoa cream
.

Harvey wallbanger

• Category: Contemporary Classics.
• Glass: highball.

Harvey wallbanger is a cocktail created any time in the US in the 50s. The name comes from the giant rabbit in the movie Harvey spoke aJames Stewart when slammed against a wall, just wallbanger in English.

Recipe:
* 3/10 vodka
* 1/10 Galliano liqueur
* 6/10 of orange juice

The cocktail is prepared directly in a glass tumbler type. The tumbler is filled with ice, vodka and orange juice according to the doses; after mixing the ingredients you add the Galliano surface. The Harvey is then decorated with an orange slice and a cherry in the glass both.

Hemingway special

- Category: Contemporary Classics.
- Glass: cocktail glass.

The Hemingway is a special cocktail afetr dinner made from light rum, grapefruit juice and maraschino. The history of this drink, became a classic, starting in Cuba in the '30s at El Floridita, the local Havana famous for its daiquiris and to be frequented by Ernest Hemingway, one of the most influential writers of the twentieth century. Hemingway, entering the bar, asked curious to try what they were drinking all present and tasted the classic daiquiri. She said it was good but it would have preferred without sugar and with double rum.
Immediately prepared him one and he exclaimed: "This is the Pope!" This is how the cocktail that bears his name: Papa Hemingway. Later, with the addition of grapefruit juice has become Hemingway special.

Recipe:
- 6 cl Rum clear
- 4 cl of grapefruit juice
- 1.5 cl Maraschino
- 1.5 cl of lime juice.

The preparation of cocktails Hemingway Special is very simple, just take the shaker and put a few ice cubes, then pour 6 cl light rum, 4 cl grapefruit juice 1.5 cl Maraschino and juice 1.5 cl lime. Once incorporated all the ingredients, shekerare vigorously and strain your cocktail in a double well chilled cocktail glass. Serve your Hemingway Special garnished with a maraschino cherry.

Horse's Neck

• Category: Contemporary Classics.
• Glass: highball.

The cocktail horse's neck is a cocktail any time based brandy and ginger ale.
The origins of this long drink dates back to 1890 and began as a non-alcoholic cocktail made up of ginger ale, ice and lemon zest. In 1910 there was a variant which was added Brandy (and sometimes the Bourbon Whiskey).

Recipe:
- 4.0 cl Brandy
- 11.0 cl Ginger Ale
- splash of Angostura bitters (optional).

It prepares directly into highball glass with ice cubes. It is mixed gently and garnish with a lemon spiral. If required, a few drops of Angostura Bitter.

Irish coffee

• Category: Contemporary Classics.
• Glass: glass Irish Coffee.

The Irish coffee or Irish coffee is a hot coffee, sugar, laced with Irish Whiskey and with a layer of cream on the surface. It served pre-heating the glass, putting the proper coffee and sweetened and adding to last the cream, lightly whipped.
Sometimes, but rarely, in the cafe they are added spices such as nutmeg or cinnamon.
The invention of the cocktail is claimed by the Irish town of Foynes, in which the bar of the port and the airport was served to warm passengers returning from transatlantic crossings. According to another tradition, the preparation of the beverage is due to Mr. Sheridan, chief barman in the bar of Shannon airport in Ireland. It was 1942, and arrived at the airport late at night and tired passengers angrily to the cancellation of their flight due to bad weather. Joe Sheridan then thought to serve them something sturdy that would refresh and "warm up" the passengers. He prepared some very strong coffee, added sugar and whiskey, completing with a topping of whipped cream. When the passengers asked him if it was Brazilian coffee, Mr. Sheridan amused replied, "No, it's Irish coffee."

Recipe:
- 2 parts cream
- 5 parts of hot coffee
- 1 teaspoon brown sugar
- 3 parts whiskey.

Take a shaker, cool them with ice, then remove it and fill it with the cream that become agitated very well for 2 minutes. This way you have got the whipped cream; put it in a bowl and place in refrigerator.
Now take a glass of Irish coffee, warm it with boiling water, pour the coffee sweetened with brown sugar, add the whiskey

and, with a spoon and without stirring, the cream previously prepared.

You can add to your Irish Coffee grated nutmeg or cinnamon.

The Irish Coffee is perfect to be enjoyed on a late winter afternoon to cool off after a long day at work or after dinner.

The Irish Coffee becomes French Coffee replacing the whiskey with brandy, Armagnac or Calvados, as it becomes American Coffee replacing the whiskey with bourbon.

Kamikaze

• Category: Drinks New Era.
• Glass: cocktail glass or tumbler for the version on the rocks.

The name already reveals the power of alcoholic cocktails. Given the versatility of the ingredients, there are a lot of versions Kamikaze (short, on the rocks, long drinks).
It is a refreshing fruity cocktails to sip on summer evenings or with the same doses divided into 4 glasses Shot, you can drink in one gulp leaving invade the digestive freshness of lemon.

Recipe:
- 4 cl of vodka
- 2 cl Cointreau or triple sec
- 1 cl lime juice
- 1 lemon peel for garnish.

Put the ice in a shaker, vodka, Cointreau and lemon juice. Shake vigorously and pour into the bowl cocktail glass filtering.
Garnish with a lemon peel curled on the edge.
Add a squirt of liquid sugar if you want a cocktail taste less acidic.
This cocktail is also available in the version on the rocks: it is achieved by putting some ice cubes in an old fashioned glass and pouring all the ingredients. Garnish with a slice of lime on the rim.
In version long drink is prepared as on the rocks, in a tall tumbler filled to the brim with soda.

Kir

• Category: Contemporary Classics.
• Glass: flute.

The kir is a cocktail-type drink, made with white wine, usually 16% alcohol.
This cocktail has French origins and legend has it that it was the abbot Kir of Dijon to propose this cocktail to guests, of course, using the French wine, a Burgundy Aligoté.
The other ingredient is the Crème de cassis, a French liqueur produced by maceration of black currant in alcohol with the addition of sugar syrup, which must have a minimum alcohol content of 15° and a content of at least 400 grams of sugar per liter. The production of this liquor is allowed only in Dijon with currants (the best variety is the Black Burgundy) collected in the Côte-d'Or.

Recipe:
- 9/10 of white wine
- 1/10 of crème de cassis (Creme de Cassis)

It is prepared directly in the flute, before pouring the Creme de Cassis and brimming with wine well chilled. Alternatively you can use a goblet for wine.
variants:
- Kir Royal - with Cremant
- Kir on the Skyy - with vodka and lime squeeze in place of wine or Champagne.
- Kir Pétillant - with sparkling wine
- Kir Imperial - with raspberries instead of currants, and Champagne.
- Kir Normand - with Normandy cider instead of white wine
- Kir Breton - with Breton cider in place of white wine
- Cidre Royal - with cider and Calvados

Lemon Drop Martini

• Category: Drinks New Era.
• Glass: Martini cup.

The Lemon Drop Martini is a cocktail any time sweet and a sour aftertaste, born in San Francisco and became famous in the 70s in California. Currently it is still one of the trendiest cocktails. Cool and refreshing, it is ideal at any time of the day.

Recipe:
- 4.5 cl Vodka
- 3 cl lemon juice + 1 lemon wedge
- 1.5 cl of sugar syrup.

Place the bowl in the freezer for a few minutes cocktails to cool.
Take it and make sure you create a crust of sugar on board.
After preparing the glass, put the ice in a shaker and pour all the ingredients, stirring well.
Serve in cocktail cup that you put aside, by filtering the content.
The edge of the cup sweetened obtained by rubbing the edge of the slice of lemon, sprinkle with sugar and letting it rest while you prepare the cocktail.
Add 1.5 cl of Cointreau or triple sec if you prefer to dampen a little 'acid cocktail.
It used a thin lemon peel for garnish the edge.

Long Island Iced Tea

• Category: Contemporary Classics.
• Glass: highball.

The Long Island Iced Tea is an after dinner cocktail made with vodka, gin, white rum and triple sec. It owes its name not to the actual presence of iced tea, but the final appearance of preparation and flavor resembling that of tea (only if the cocktail is prepared with the right amount of each ingredient).
Born during the American Prohibition during which alcohol was banned and alcohol was smuggled as tea infusion.

Recipe:
- 1.5 cl Vodka
- 1.5 cl White Rum
- 1.5 cl Triple sec
- 1.5 cl Tequila
- 1.5 cl Gin
- 2.5 cl fresh lemon juice
- 3 cl sugar syrup
- 1 top of Cola

Take a glass type highball or high ball and fill it with ice cubes. Pour on the rocks 1.5 cl of vodka, 1.5 cl White Rum, 1.5 cl Gin, 1.5 cl Tequila, 1.5 cl of triple sec.
Then add 2.5 cl fresh lemon juice and 3 cl sugar syrup. Fill the glass to the brim with cola. Mix gently. Garnish with a spiral of lemon or lime. Serve with a straw.

Variants:
- Long Beach Iced Tea: replacing the cola with cranberry juice.
- Beverly Hills Iced Tea: replacing the cola with champagne.
- Miami Iced Tea: replacing the cola with lemonade and triple sec with blue Curacao.

- Georgia Peach Iced Tea or Iced Tea: replacing the triple sec with Peach tree.
- Japanese Iced Tea: replacing the cola with lemonade and triple sec with melon liqueur (usually midori).
- Italian Iced Tea: replacing the triple sec with amaretto (usually Di Saronno).
- Mexican Iced Tea: replacing the triple sec and tequila and cola with tonic water.

Mai Tai

• Category: Contemporary Classics.
• Glass: highball.

The Mai Tai is an alcoholic cocktail after dinner made with rum, curacao and lime juice, associated with the Polynesian culture.
It is credited with the invention at Trader Vic's restaurant in Oakland, California, in 1944. The local rival Don the Beachcomber he claims the invention making it back to 1933, although the recipes of the two rooms are different.
Its name in Tahitian language means simply good, because you do not need to say more.
The Mai Tai is a very alcoholic cocktails, powerful, dry, fruity with a good background, but where the flavor of rum, light and dark, is predominant.
For a Mai Thai perfect, the quality of the rum is essential.

Recipe:
- 4 cl of white rum
- 2 cl dark rum
- 1.5 cl of orange curacao
- 1.5 cl orgeat syrup
- 1 cl fresh lime juice.

All ingredients except the dark rum are shaken in a shaker with ice. Is poured into the glass, there is the additional dark rum making stratify surface.
It is served on the rocks in a glass high ball.
Seal umbrella paper.

Manhattan

• Category: The Unforgettables.
• Glass: Martini cup.

Manhattan is one of the most famous cocktail made with whiskey; it serves as an aperitif (before dinner). It is said that the inventor of this drink was a bartender at the Manhattan Club in New York (hence the name), that would prepare him for the first time in 1874.
The proportions of whiskey and sweet vermouth vary from 1: 1 to a dry 4: 1, but according to some sources, the original recipe was 2: 1 and was used only Rye whiskey. Over time they have changed is the recipe ingredients, so much so that the most popular version in the United States today uses whiskey.
The qualities of most common are rye whiskey, Canadian whiskey and bourbon.

Recipe:
- 5.0 cl Rye or Canadian whiskey
- 2.0 cl of red vermouth
- 1 drop of Angostura.

The Manhattan is prepared by mixing (not shaken) ingredients in the mixing glass filled with ice to 2/3. (Note that the angostura tastes very pronounced, could be enough only one drop, according to taste.)
Serve in a cocktail glass (from "Martini"), garnished with a maraschino cherry.

Margarita

• Category: Contemporary Classics.
• Glassware: double cocktail glass or cup sombrero.

The Margarita is the most common Mexican cocktail made with tequila, and belongs to sour. In Latin "margarita" it meant pearl in Spanish is the translation of the word daisy.
According to reports by William Grimes, author of Straight Up or On the Rocks: The Story of the American Cocktail, many people claim to have been drinking margarita in Mexico already in the thirties, which implies that the Margarita was not invented after 1940.

The proportions are more used to the Margarita;
* 2: 1: 1 (50% tequila, triple sec 25%, 25% fresh lime or lemon juice).
* 3: 2: 1 (50% tequila, Triple Sec 33%, 17% fresh lime or lemon juice).
* 3: 1: 1 (60% tequila, Triple Sec 20%, 20% fresh lime or lemon juice).
* 1: 1: 1 (33% tequila, Triple Sec 33%, 33% fresh lime or lemon juice).

although the standard IBA Official Cocktail is:
* 7: 4: 3 (50% tequila, Triple Sec 28.5%, 21.5% fresh lime or lemon juice).

The drink is usually served shaken with ice, "on the rocks" or mixed with ice (the "frozen margarita"); in the classic recipe it is served in the typical cup called Sombrero or double cup cocktail. The cocktail is often served with salt on the glass rim ("Crusta").
Although the most common Margarita contain tequila, orange liqueur, lime juice or lemon, and sometimes an additional sweetener, many variations are becoming increasingly common.
Use bottled lime juice (containing sugar) is another way used to sweeten the cocktail.
You can also add fruit juice to Margarita. Typical examples are the following combinations:

- lime juice with cranberry.
- strawberry or peach, lemon juice;.
- banana with banana juice.

However, it is important to point out that Margarita with fruit are not part of the definition of a classic "Margarita".

Mary Pickford

• Category: The Unforgettables.
• Glassware: double cocktail glass.

The Mary Pickford is a delicious cocktail from ladies born in America in the thirties. Also this is one of the precursors, along with Bacardi and the Daiquiri, the mixed drinks with rum and fruit juice.

The inventor devised it inspired by the famous American actress Mary Pickford, who lived between 1893 and 1979, known as the "America's Sweetheart".

This cocktail evokes the scents of the Caribbean, thanks to the combination of rum and blended fruit juices and is ideal to be enjoyed in the afternoon served in double cup; if, however, increased a little dose of pineapple juice and serve in lowball, it becomes an excellent long drink for any time of day.

Recipe:
- 6 cl White rum
- 1 cl Maraschino
- 6 cl pineapple juice
- 1 cl grenadine syrup.

The Mary Pickford prepares elaborate using the shaker and a glass goblet. First pour the crushed ice in a shaker, pineapple juice, grenadine, maraschino and rum. Then vigorously shake the shaker and then poured, filtering the content using the special pass, in the glass. Finally garnish putting on a cocktail skewer a piece of pineapple and a cherry.

Mimosa

• Category: Contemporary Classics.
• Glass: flute.

The Mimosa is a variant of the cocktail Bellini, Rossini and Tintoretto.
Also called Buck's fizz is part of the category of medium drink, although when preparing Buck's fizz is put a smaller percentage of champagne or prosecco and more orange juice.
When you add the Grand Marnier, then called Grand Mimosa.

Recipe:
- 7.5 cl of orange juice
- 7.5 cl of Prosecco.

Pour the orange juice into a champagne flute with sparkling wine (you can also use Champagne). Mix gently. You can garnish with an orange twist.
The ideal time to enjoy it are the winter months, when in fact the fruits ripen. The Buck's fizz was created by Mr. McGarry, bartender at Buck's Club in London in 1921.

Mint Julep

• Category: Contemporary Classics.
• Glass: tumbler.

The mint julep is a cocktail originating in the United States of South-based mint and Bourbon whiskey type.
Mint just means mint julep is a term that derives from and gulab means water (ab) for roses (gul) and by extension indicates an aqueous syrup sweet and fragrant mint.
So mint julep is a sweet syrup of mint, with the addition of crushed ice and Bourbon. You may think the mint julep probably as a Bourbon with mint granita and garnished with mint leaves, in order to stimulate the sense of smell.

Recipe:
- Some fresh mint leaves
- 1 tablespoon sugar
- Ground ice
- 7.5 cl. bourbon.

In a tumbler or a glass old fashion put the mint and sugar with a tablespoon of water. Pounded leaves and sugar with a pestle until all the sugar has melted. Now filled the glass with crushed ice, pour the whiskey, stir and serve garnished with a sprig of mint.
Being a refreshing drink and a cocktail in the amount of alcohol should be minimal in order to have a total alcohol content about how the classic Italian refreshing drink, made with lots of water and a little wine. Clearly, being able to vary at will the amount of mint, Bourbon and water, there is a classically trained but then everyone does the mint julep by varying the amount of the ingredients depending on your taste. Traditionally, the mint julep was served in silver or pewter cup but today they are used glasses like "old style" (Old Fashioned glass, lowball glass, rocks or glass) short and wide or in a glass tumbler type called Collins glass , high and wide or in a Highball glass a middle way between the two previous.

Mojito

• Category: Contemporary Classics.
• Glass: highball.

The mojito is a popular cocktail any time of Cuban origin consisting of rum, sugar, lime juice, mint leaves (hierba buena in Cuba) and sparkling water.
The origin of the mojito remains quite controversial: it is often told that a cocktail similar to moijto was invented by the famous English pirate Sir Francis Drake in the fourteenth century.
That version was prepared with aguardiente (rum unaged) low quality, lime, water, refined white sugar cane and a local species of mint, hierba buena (the hierba buena in Cuba is an herb that is easy spontaneous, its flavor is more delicate and less persistent wild mint or mint that is located in Europe).
In mid-1800 it seems that the company Bacardi has boosted popularity of the drink, which in any case will reach its ultimate popularity only in the twentieth century.
Also on the modern version of the mojito does not seem to be absolutely certain of who proposed it first, even if the names are usually more pronounced than those of the barman Bodeguita del Medio, Attilio De La Fuente, or Angel Martinez, who actually took over the club in 1942, at the height of his fame to be attended by famous personalities such as Ernest Hemingway, known consumer of the drink and that with his statement, also written in the local "My mojito in La Bodeguita, My daiquiri in El Floridita" made famous drink even outside of Cuba.

Recipe:
* 5 cl of white rum Cuban
* lime
* 2 teaspoons brown sugar refined white
* 6-8 mint leaves
* Ice cubes
* carbonated water (or water of Seltz or soda).

It is prepared by placing on the bottom of the glass two teaspoons of white cane sugar and the juice of half a lime.

The ingredients are blended together and at this point is added mint which should not be pounded but only lightly pressed and mixed together with the juice and sugar (this arrangement means that the mint does not give off the bitter notes).

Later it joins the ice, white rum (Havana Club or 3 years) and finally the sparkling water. The mixture is then served with a straw and a sprig of mint decoration.

The only option allowed in Cuba is the final addition of Angostura, so you get a "Mojito Criollo".

The Mojitaly is another variation of the Mojito, which involves the use (in place of rum) of Branca Menta.

A refreshing cocktail, presented as a long drink, to drink ideally from spring onwards. Instead of lime you can also include the use of the mapo, a citrus hybrid between tangerine and grapefruit.

Recipe:
- 4 cl Fernet Mint
- 3 cl lime juice or mapo
- 3 sprigs of mint
- 2 cane sugar
- Soda Water

Slightly crush the mint, sugar and lime juice (you can substitute with mapo).
Add the crushed ice and soda.
Garnish with mint and lime twist.
Serve with straws.

There is also a non-alcoholic version of the Mojito, which is generally called "Virgin Mojito", where the rum is replaced by gas (sprite, seven-up) or ginger-ale.

Monkey Gland

• Category: The Unforgettables.
• Glass: cocktail glass.

The Monkey Gland is an all day cocktail made with gin, orange juice, grenadine and absinthe.
Its name means "monkey gland" and seems to have been devised by the barman Harry MacElhone, at Harry's New York Bar in Paris, in honor of the scientist Serge Voronoff.
The name refers to the testicles of monkey: Voronoff had developed a practice which involved the installation of monkey testicular tissue of humans with the intent to rejuvenate the patient.

Recipe:
* 5 cl of gin
* 3 cl fresh orange juice
* 2 drops of absinthe
* 2 drops of grenadine

Take a cocktail glass and cool it by filling it with ice cubes. In a second glass add 5 cl of gin, then 3 cl fresh orange juice, 2 drops of grenadine and 2 drops of absinthe.
Pour into a shaker filled with ice and shake well.
Serve without straw.

Moscow mule

• Category: Contemporary Classics.
• Glass: highball.

The Moscow Mule is one of the most famous cocktails ever, a pillar of the history of mixed.
The Moscow is a long drink with an alcohol content not too high, the refreshing drink par excellence, the famously pungent ginger.
This cocktail is the result of a happy discovery two made in 1941, when an employee of a company that makes soft drinks and the owner of a bar in Los Angeles had to find a solution on the use of surplus stocks of ginger.

Recipe:
- 3 cl vodka
- 8 cl ginger-ale or ginger-beer
- 1 cl lemon juice
- a few leaves of fresh mint
- a few slices of cucumber
- a slice of lime as decoration.

Put crushed ice in a shaker and add the vodka and lime juice, shaking the shaker so not cool. Pour into a hurricane or in a highball glass and fill with ginger.
Garnish with a slice of lime and serve with a straw.

Negroni

• Category: The Unforgettables.
• Glass: tumbler.

The Negroni is a pre-dinner cocktail alcohol typical dark orange, made with red vermouth, bitter Campari and gin.
It was created in Florence in 1920 by Count Camillo Negroni. In the 20s the Count attending aristocratic Coffee Casoni in Via de 'Tornabuoni in Florence and, tired of the usual aperitif American, asked the barman Fosco Scarselli, a dash of gin instead of soda at his last travel to the US in honor of London .
What the count was "the usual", became for others an "American stylish Count Negroni" or an American with an addition of gin and took the name of the count who loved him so much.
Today the Negroni is considered one of the most famous Italian aperitif, and around the world is known simply as "Negroni".

Recipe:
- 3 cl gin
- 3 cl Campari bitters
- 3 cl of sweet red vermouth
- Half orange slice.

Cool an old fashioned glass with ice, once cold drain the water with a strainer.
The recipe IBA recommend preparing the drink into the glass "On the rocks", pouring 3 cl London dry gin, 3 cl of bitter Campari and red vermouth 3 cl. Then gently stir with a bar spoon.
Complete with half a slice (or rind squeezed) orange. Serve without straw.

A variant is the Negroni "wrong", which differs from the classic Negroni for the presence of brut sparkling wine, which replaces the gin. The drink becomes lighter thanks to the lower presence of alcohol.

Another variant is the RedHuvber, a cocktail that comes from changing the Negroni, which is replaced in the version aperitif Campari bitters with campari soda, making the slightly fizzy cocktails and lighter; It is served on the rocks and in an old fashioned glass.

Old Fashioned

• Category: The Unforgettables.
• Glass: tumbler.

The Old Fashioned is a pre-dinner cocktail made with bourbon in which they are dissolved sugar, angostura bitters and essence of orange peel. It is so named because it is served in glasses just called old fashioned (tumbler).

Recipe:
- 4.5 cl bourbon or rye whiskey
- 2 drops of Angostura bitters
- 1 sugar cube
- 1 splash of soda
- Garnish: slice of orange and a cherry

- Take a glass like old fashioned from 6.10 fluid ounces, ask you a sugar cube and soak it with drops of Angostura (1.8-2.5 ml). Use a pestle to crush the lump. Add a dash of natural water to dissolve the sugar and mix better be careful not to create lumps and obtain a homogeneous solution.
- Add an ounce of bourbon and then 3-4 ice cubes. Use the bar spoon to mix and dissolve the sugar (and possibly syrup) in bourbon.
- Add more ice cubes up to fill the glass, then another ounce of bourbon. Mix again with the bar spoon. Get with a vegetable peeler a long slice of orange peel over the glass so that the orange essence settles in the solution and the perfume. You can also crush slightly above the glass to obtain the result.
- Cut and clean the slice of orange zest, then add it to cocktails. Enter a maraschino cherry in the cocktail and get an orange slice garnish with which the glass.
- Serve without straw.

Paradise

• Category: The Unforgettables.
• Glass: cocktail glass.

The Paradise is an after dinner cocktail made with gin and apricot brandy.

The aromatic flavor of gin is softened sweetness of brandy, which in turn finds balance and freshness in the orange juice. A game of flavors that alternate in a tangle hot and cold, fresh and pungent, but always pleasant.

It drinks suitable for all occasions, compact and always to be proposed as after dinner or for diners not yet accustomed to cocktails more challenging, but not difficult trovarà admirers.

Of "Paradise Cocktail" great little is known and according to some sources, the only historical record dates back to the owner's Harry Craddock of 1930. Moreover, it is argued that the cocktail was born in England in the '20s at the hands of a stranger, but few would maintain that it was Harry Craddock to create it.

Recipe:
- 3.5 cl gin
- 2 cl apricot brandy (apricot brandy)
- 1.5 cl of orange juice

Fill a cocktail glass with ice to cool it. Fill a shaker with ice, take off the excess water, then add 3.5 cl of gin, apricot brandy and 2 cl 1.5 cl of fresh orange juice and shake well.

Filter the contents of the shaker into a cocktail glass emptied of ice. Serve without straw.

Piña Colada

• Category: Contemporary Classics.
• Glass: highball.

The Piña Colada is a very sweet after dinner cocktail made with light rum, coconut milk and pineapple juice (or pineapple chunks), a native of Puerto Rico, where the country is said to have been created for the first time in 1963 by Don Ramon Portas Mingot, that trying to conceive an original cocktail made with fruit, prepared the first Coladas. In Old San Juan is a marble commemorative plaque to commemorate this event.

Recipe:
   • 60 ml white rum
   • 30 ml of Coconut Cream
   • 90 ml pineapple juice.

Put crushed ice in a shaker, rum, coconut cream and pineapple juice.
Shake gently.
Remember not to completely melt the ice, they must remain fragments.
Then served in a highball glass with a cherry or a slice of pineapple.

The Chi Chi is identical to piña colada except for rum that is replaced with vodka.

Pisco sour

• Category: Drinks New Era.
• Glass: flute or champagne glass.

The Pisco Sour is a cocktail made with pisco whose invention is attributed to Victor Morris, American immigrant in Salt Lake City who moved to Peru in 1913. After an initial period spent working for the Cerro de Pasco Railroad, Victor opened the Morris Bar in downtown Lima that became in no time hangout upper-class Peruvian immigrant and native English speakers.
Morris began serving Pisco Sour in his bar as an alternative to the Whiskey Sour cocktail and continued to maintain popularity even after the death of Morris in 1929.
Although its origin is disputed by Chile, it is therefore clear that the cocktail was born in Peru.
The Pisco Sour is the national drink of Peru where even a national holiday is celebrated on the first Saturday of February.

Recipe:
- 40 grams of pisco (brandy in South America)
- Juice of half a lemon
- 1/2 tablespoon sugar
- egg white
- Amargo Chuncho Bitter
- Ice cubes

It is prepared in a shaker shaking vigorously. In a shaker is put egg whites and the cocktails are made down four drops of Amargo Chuncho Bitter.
It is suggested maximum two ice cubes per person.

Planter's Punch

- Category: The Unforgettables.
- Glass: highball.

Punch, meaning drink made of rum (light or dark is indifferent) and juice, it is one of the most popular cocktails any time in the Caribbean region. Surely it is one of the oldest: apparently was drunk by the owners of the plantations of sugar cane and their slaves already in the seventeenth century, because of the easy availability of the ingredients in those territories. The punch is a cocktail rather easy to prepare and that we can give free rein to the taste and imagination by mixing different fruits.

Recipe:
- 4.5 cl Dark rum
- 3.5 cl of orange juice
- 3.5 cl of pineapple juice
- 2 cl lemon juice
- 1 cl grenadine
- 1 cl of liquid sugar
- 3 or 4 dashes Angostura.

Place all ingredients, except the Angostura, in a shaker filled with ice and shake.
Strain and pour into a highball glass filled with ice. Add the Angostura end preparation.
Garnish with maraschino cherry and pineapple slice.
If desired, you can replace the pineapple juice with passion fruit, kiwi, strawberry, tangerine, peach.

Porto flip

• Category: The Unforgettables.
• Glass: cocktail glass.

Flip the Porto is part of the family of "flip", ie those cocktails egg and frothy. Energy drinks are usually made from liquor, sugar and egg. The base of the port itself has a slight alcohol content, the addition of brandy makes a little more consistent, making it a great accompaniment for dry desserts, or for an after dinner winter (after dinner cocktail).

Recipe:
- 1.5 cl of brandy
- 4 cl Port wine
- 1 cl egg yolk.

It is prepared by placing all ingredients in a shaker with addition of ice. Serve in a cocktail glass. Finally sprinkle nutmeg on the surface.

Ramos Fizz

- Category: The Unforgettables.
- Glass: lowball.

It is a drink with a long history, dating back to 1888 and a unique taste, which hardly meets in almost every other drink. The trick to the Ramos Gin Fizz is to create a stable foam, with albumen (egg white) and cream. This classic was created by Henry C. Ramos in 1888, in his bar in New Orleans, was originally called "New Orleans Fizz".
Before Prohibition this drink was very popular. The drink was so popular and request that it was difficult for the bartender to keep up with orders.

Recipe:
- 4.5 cl gin
- 1.5 cl fresh lemon juice
- 1.5 cl fresh lime juice
- 3 cl simple syrup
- 6 cl of cream (heavy cream)
- 3 drops of orange flower water
- 2 drops of vanilla extract
- 1 egg white
- soda

Take a collins, add 4.5 cl Gin 1.5 cl fresh lemon juice 1.5 cl fresh lime juice and simple syrup 3 cl. Then, add three drops of orange flower water, then a few drops of vanilla extract. Add 6 cl of cream (heavy cream) and the egg white of an egg.
Put everything in a shaker without ice and shake for 3 minutes, then repeat the operation by filling it with ice. In theory it should agitate for a total of 12 minutes. Pour into collins glass without ice.
Then add soda to the brim of the glass. Serve with a straw.

Rose

• Category: Contemporary Classics.
• Glass: cocktail glass.

The cocktail Rose, was born in Paris in the 20s precisely from the hands of the bartender Johnny Mitta the Chatham Bar in Paris.
In addition to the original story regarding the birth of Rose cocktail, there is also a form of legend in which it is said that this cocktail was born around 1445 during the "War of the Roses" fought between Lancaster whose emblem was a red rose , and the house of York, symbolized by a white rose, but is not believed to be a true story.
Its blend makes it a light aperitif (before dinner) and delicate, as delicate is the color wearing a pale pink due to liquor kirsch and cherry brandy.

Recipe:
- 4.5 dry vermouth
- 1.0 cl of cherry brandy
- 1.5 cl of Kirsch.

Shake with ice and strain into a cocktail glass. Garnish with a cocktail cherry.

Russian Spring Punch

• Category: Drinks New Era.
• Glass: highball.

The Russian Spring Punch is a cocktail created by Dick Bradsell.
According to his account, there was a party where everyone
drank Champagne. That's how Bradsell decides to mix vodka,
lemon, sugar and cream de cassis with ice, to offer it to guests.
The same Bradsell says that wandering between the various
local, many had made of variants, but this drink as well as he has
proposed is balanced, while replacing an ingredient or change
the dose, that does not get a drink completely different.

Recipe:
* 2.5 cl Vodka
* 2.5 cl Lemon juice
* 1.5 cl Crème de Cassis
* 1 cl sugar syrup.

Shake all ingredients. Pour into the glass high ball and fill with
sparkling wine. Garnish with a slice of lemon and blackberries.

Rusty Nail

- Category: The Unforgettables.
- Glass: tumbler.

The Rusty Nail is an after dinner cocktail made with Drambuie and Scotch whiskey. Made with whiskey and Drambuie, the Rusty Nail is a very strong cocktail taste rough, as his name indicates, rusty, in Italian "rusty". From Scotland is a great accompaniment to a chat between friends.

Recipe:
- 4.5 cl Scotch whiskey
- 2.5 cl Drambuie (honey liqueur).

Place the ingredients directly in a glass of old fashioned kind with ice and add lemon rind rolled (lemon twist in English).
The Drambuie is Scotch Whisky flavored with heather honey and herbs.
It is said to be prepared according to the traditional nanny Charles.

Sazerac

• Category: The Unforgettables.
• Glass: tumbler.

The Sazerac was born in the mid-1800s, in the charming New Orleans, at the time real Mecca for cocktails and alcoholic pleasures. Prepare the Sazerac is a ritual, not only because it is one of the oldest in the history of cocktail drink, but also for its composition, which includes ingredients sought and mysterious as absinthe and Peychaud's bitters.
The recipe is simple: cognac, a sugar cube soaked in 2 drops of bitters and absinthe, a few drops of this elixir to give an aura of magic to drink. The result is cocktail enveloping scent and hypnotic, full of references herbaceous and suggestive that weave warm charm of cognac. The palate is majestic, warm, with bitter notes that draw a myriad of shades purple.

Recipe:
- 5 cl of cognac
- 1 cl absinthe
- 1 sugar cube
- 2 drops of Peychaud's bitters

1. Put the ice in a glass, wait for it to be well cooled and then pour absinthe, which cover the sides of the glass, perfectly, and add more ice.
2. In another glass put sugar cube soaked in bitters and work with the pestle and a few drops of water. Pour ice and then cognac.
3. Discard the ice and any excess absinthe and then pour the cocktail filtering.
4. The taste of absinthe is very strong, so be careful to leave just a caress green, otherwise the fine balance of the cocktail is ruined.
5. Garnish with a lemon peel. If you want you can also crush the peel to infuse the drink a subtle hint of citrus.

Screwdriver

- Category: The Unforgettables.
- Glass: highball.

Screwdriver is an after dinner cocktail made with vodka and orange juice, which belongs to the category of long drinks with an alcohol content oscillating around 15%.
Screwdriver, also called "vodka-orange" is a classic, super required, timeless, that lends itself to an endless number of variations and suitable for every type of palate because of its simplicity.
His name, which in Italian means "screwdriver", reminds us of his documented history when, in the mid-twentieth century, American engineers abroad used to, for convenience, use their screwdrivers to mix cocktails.

Recipe:
- 5 cl (1 part) vodka
- 10 cl (2 parts) orange juice.

Mix the vodka and orange juice in a shaker and strain into a highball glass with an orange peel.

Sea breeze

• Category: Contemporary Classics.
• Glass: highball.

This is a typical summer cocktail (sea breeze), also thanks to the availability of seasonal ingredients.
Vodka and fruit juice are a winning combination found in many drinks.
There is also a variant Hawaiian, the Bay breeze, with pineapple juice instead of grapefruit juice.
The cocktail dates back to the twenties, but it seems that the original recipe was different from that used today: for example gin and grenadine took the place of the vodka and grapefruit juice.

Recipe:
- 4.0 cl of vodka
- 12.0 cl cranberry juice red
- 3.0 cl of grapefruit juice.

Pour ingredients into a glass type high ball, filled with ice. Garnish, finally, with a slice of lime and serve with two straws.

Sex on the Beach

• Category: Contemporary Classics.
• Glass: highball.

Sex on the beach is perhaps one of the most drunk cocktails any time in Europe. Born before the fun on the beach and then the peach on the beach, it consists of 2 cl vodka 2 cl midori, 2 cl Chambord, pineapple juice and cranberry, which had the effect of darkening enormously cocktail and give him a very sweet taste. However the European continent, in the early eighties, the midori was not readily available, so it is the formula of the initial fun on the beach to establish itself in Europe, then changing its name to the current one: sex on the beach.

Recipe:
  • 1/2 part of Vodka
  • Vodka 1/2 part of the fishing
  • 1 part cranberry juice
  • 1 part of juice Orange
  • 1 part pineapple juice (optional)
  • a cherry and a slice of pineapple to decorate
  • 3 ice cubes.

Put ice cubes in a shaker, add Vodka, Vodka peach, orange juice and pineapple juice if you want. Shake until it cools down the shaker.
Pour into a highball adding cranberry juice, decorated with a cherry or a slice of pineapple and serve with a straw. The special feature of the preparation of this cocktail is to pour the cranberry juice at the end, and absolutely without stirring: the goal is to create an original chromatic contrast making the light color of the drink against the dark color of blackcurrant juice that, when paid, decreasing gradually to the bottom, creating the desired effect.

Sidecar

• Category: The Unforgettables.
• Glass: cocktail glass.

The Sidecar is a classic cocktail after dinner, traditionally prepared with cognac, orange liqueur (Cointreau, Grand Marnier or other triple sec), and lemon juice.
While not peaceful the exact origin of the Sidecar, it is believed to have been invented at the Hotel Ritz in Paris towards the end of World War II.
Later it became famous thanks to Harry Mc Halone founder of Harry's Bar, also in Paris, who dedicated this cocktail to an eccentric captain who came in with all his sidecar in the bar driven by his driver.

Recipe:
- Eight parties of brandy or cognac
- Two parts of Cointreau
- A portion of lemon juice.

Mix the ingredients in a shaker half filled with ice. Strain and serve in a cocktail glass with sugared rim. Garnish with a strip of lemon peel or orange.

Singapore Sling

• Category: Contemporary Classics.
• Glass: highball.

The Singapore Sling is a cocktail any time created in 1915 by Ngiam Tong Boon, bartender Raffles Hotel in Singapore.

Recipe:
  • 3 cl gin
  • 1.5 cl Heering Cherry Liqueur
  • 0.75 cl of triple sec
  • 0.75 cl DOM Benedictine
  • 1 cl grenadine
  • 12 cl of juice 'pineapple
  • 1.5 cl fresh lime juice
  • 1 dash of Angostura

In the glass of preparation add 3 cl Gin, 1.5 cl Heering Cherry Liqueur, 0.75 cl of triple sec, 0.75 cl Benedictine, 1 cl grenadine, lime juice 1.5 cl, 12 cl pineapple juice, a splash of Angostura.
Pour into a shaker filled with ice and shake.
Filter into a glass high ball previously filled with ice. Garnish with a slice of pineapple and a maraschino cherry.

Spritz

• Category: Drinks New Era.
• Glass: tumbler.

Spritz is an alcoholic aperitif Italian, popular in the Triveneto, based Prosecco, sparkling water or seltzer and, in the alternative, stained with bitters.
The origins are unknown, but among the population of Venice is said that a considerable part in the spread of the spritz have had the soldiers of the Austrian Empire, stationed in what was formerly the Republic of Venice and then became part of the Kingdom of Lombardy -Veneto, which, to dilute the high alcohol content of wines from Veneto, they would be stretched with sparkling water; hence the origin of the name you want, you want to derive from the German verb Austrian spritzen, which means "spray", the gesture just to stretch the wine with sparkling water.

Recipe:
  • 6 cl Prosecco
  • 4 cl Aperol or other bitter choice
  • A splash of soda / seltzer.

Pour into an old-fashioned glass (tumbler), containing ice, prosecco, Aperol and finally the soda, stir. Garnish with half orange slice.

Stinger

- Category: The Unforgettables.
- Glass: tumbler.

The Stinger is an after dinner cocktail made with cognac.
The cocktail was born in the early last century but became famous in the United States at the time of Prohibition as masked mint liqueur.
The Stinger is a cocktail that includes his name in his being and his glory, accompanying him since the day of his birth. Stinger The term derives from the verb "Sting" which means stinging, itching, burning, as if the man who devised it wanted to understand the effect that this brings short drink when ingested.
Its blend is in fact a mix of cognac and cream of mint, it gives the cocktail its intense flavor and persistent taking it to be one of the best digestive ever.

Recipe:
- 7/10 Brandy
- 3/10 Creme de Menthe white.

The ingredients in a shaker with ice cubes. Serve in a glass tumbler.
The version with vodka instead of Brandy is called Vodka Stinger or White Spider.

Tequila Sunrise

Category: Contemporary Classics.
Glass: highball.

A drink sour and slightly strengthened by the presence of tequila that can be appreciated even by those who drink less alcohol. The tequila sunrise cocktail any time is one of the most common but popular at the same time: in fact, in 1973 the Eagles devoted a single of the same name and then, in 1988, trod the scenes of the film thanks to the homonymous production of a film by Mel Gibson and Michelle Pfeiffer.

Recipe:
- 4.5 cl tequila
- 9 cl Orange Juice
- 1.5 cl grenadine syrup
- Seal: half orange slice and maraschino cherry.

Prepare a high ball glass with ice. Pour the tequila, orange juice and then pour grenadine syrup. The grenadine will settle to the bottom giving the drink effect sunrise (dawn). Complete with half a slice of orange and a cocktail cherry.

Tom Collins

• Category: The Unforgettables.
• Glass: lowball.

The Tom Collins is a afetr dinner cocktail, a long drink made of "Old Tom Gin" (a sweetened version of gin, forerunner of London Dry Gin), lemon juice, sugar and soda that is served with ice (on the rocks) in wide glasses.

Recipe:
- 4.5 cl of Old Tom Gin
- 3 cl fresh lemon juice
- 1.5 sugar syrup
- 6 cl soda
- 1 slice of lemon
- 1 maraschino cherry.

Take a glass lowball and sit a lemon to get an ounce of juice.
Add half an ounce of sugar syrup and an ounce and a half of dry gin (Old Tom Gin). Fill the glass to the brim with ice cubes.
Pour into a shaker and shake, then pour into collins glass.
Add soda to the brim of the glass. Garnish with a slice of lemon or lime and a maraschino cherry.
Serve without straw.

Variations of Tom Collins differ primarily in the base used.
- Brandy Collins - with brandy
- Jack Collins - with apple jack
- John Collins - with 1.5 ounces of rye whiskey (varieties of whiskey US) or bourbon instead of gin. The IBA recipe involves adding 3-4 drops of Angostura. It is perhaps best known variant of Tom Collins.
- Michael Collins - with Irish whiskey, in honor of the Irish leader Michael Collins
- Ron Collins - with rum
- Sam Collins - with gin
- Sandy Collins or Jock Collins - with Scotch whiskey

- Vodka Collins or Comrade Collins - with vodka
- Pedro Collins - with rum
- José Collins - with tequila
- Phil Collins - with tequila, Irish whiskey, vodka, rum, beer and, in honor of Phil Collins.

Tommy's Margarita

- Category: Drinks New Era.
- Glass: cocktail glass.

The Tommy's Margarita is a cocktail any time, a variation of the Margarita, the most common Mexican cocktail made with tequila.

It seems that Tommy's Margarita is designed by Julio Bermejo considered by many to be a world expert on Tequila and "ambassador" of Tequila in the United States. This particular variant of the more famous Margarita, started in 1980 to be served at the restaurant of his father, the legendary Tommy's World's Best Restaurant and Tequila Bar in San Francisco.

This restaurant was opened by Tommy Elmy Bermejo with his wife, in 1965. They pledged to serve guests the true Mexican and Yucatan, but above all the local houses the largest collection of 100% agave tequila outside Mexico almost 300 bottles.

Son Julio spent many years behind the counter, contributing to the spread of Tequila among patrons.

Recipe:
- 4.5 cl Tequila
- 1.5 cl fresh lime juice
- 2 teaspoons of agave nectar.

Shake and strain into a chilled cocktail cocktails.

Tuxedo

• Category: The Unforgettables.
• Glass: cocktail glass.

The Tuxedo is an all day cocktail made with gin, dry vermouth, maraschino, absinthe and orange bitters.
Tuxedo is the term with which the Americans refer to our tuxedo, ie what is the most elegant dress.
This cocktail is thought to have been created by Harry Johnson recipe was published for the first time since "Bartenders Manual" in 1882.
The drink was created at the Tuxedo Club as is often said, because that opened in 1886 (four years later). While the club can not claim to have created this cocktail, it is credited with being the birthplace of the tuxedo (dress).

Recipe:
- 3 cl Gin (Old Tom Gin)
- 3 cl dry vermouth
- 2.5 ml (half a bar spoon) maraschino
- 1 ml (quarter of a bar spoon) of absinthe
- 1 ml (quarter of a bar spoon) of orange bitters

Take a cocktail glass and fill it with ice to cool it. Fill a second glass of ice, then add 3 cl gin 3 cl dry vermouth, maraschino 2.5 ml, 1 ml of wormwood and 1 ml of orange bitters.
Mix well, then strain into a chilled cocktail after removing the ice. Lightly squeeze a slice of lemon peel over the glass, then garnish with the same slice spiral and with a cherry cocktail. Serve without straw.

Vampiro

• Category: Drinks New Era.
• Glass: highball.

It is an original cocktail, absolutely unconventional usual drinking. Energy, invigorating, suitable for those who love the tomato and especially the strong flavors. It can be served as an aperitif or to replenish minerals.

Recipe:
- 5 cl Tequila (silver)
- 7 cl Tomato juice
- 3 cl Fresh orange juice
- 1 cl fresh lime juice
- 1 teaspoon clear honey
- Half slice of onion, finely chopped.
- A little bit of fresh chili
- A few drops Worcestershire sauce
- Salt

Pour all ingredients into a cocktail shaker with ice. Shake well to release some 'juice chilli. Strain into a high ball with ice and garnish with a slice of lime and chili peppers (green or red).

Vesper

• Category: Drinks New Era.
• Glass: cocktail glass.

Vesper and Vesper Martini is a cocktail consisting of gin, vodka and Kina Lillet (the latter now called Lillet Blanc). It is part of the category of pre-dinner cocktail.
The cocktail was invented in 1953 by Ian Fleming's novel Casino Royale. The secret agent James Bond order and appoints the cocktail party in honor of Vesper Lynd, Bondgirl of which 007 were in love.

Recipe:
- three pieces of Gordon's gin: 4.5 cl
- a part of vodka 1,5 cl
- middle part of Kina Lillet (now out of print, using the Lillet Blanc): 0.75 cl
- a long, thin slice of lemon peel.

Shake ingredients with ice in a shaker and strain into a chilled cocktail glass, garnish with a long, thin slice of lemon peel.

Whisky Sour

• Category: The Unforgettables.
• Glass: tumbler.

Whiskey Sour is a cocktail any time based bourbon whiskey with lemon juice, sugar and egg white.

Recipe:
* 45 ml of Bourbon Whiskey
* 22 ml of fresh lemon juice
* 15 ml sugar syrup
* 1 splash of liqueur all'Arancia
* 1 egg white of egg
* Ice q.s.
* A splash of essential oils contained in an orange peel.

Squeeze 22 ml lemon juice then add 15 ml of syrup. Add 45 ml of bourbon. Then proceed with the addition of an egg white. Put the solution in a shaker and shake firmly.
Fill the shaker with ice and then stir again all. Pour the solution of the shaker into a glass type old fashioned or cobbler previously filled to the brim with ice cubes.
Garnish with half orange slice on the glass and a maraschino cherry. Serve without straw.

White lady

• Category: The Unforgettables.
• Glass: cocktail glass.

The White Lady is simple and elegant. And classy. The White Lady is a cocktail after dinner International, a Short Drink dry taste and light that will fill yourself with the freshness of its lemon flavor. Many countries claim paternity. France says that it was created in honor of the opera "La Dame invisible" by François-Adrien Boieldieu; the United States according to which it was dedicated to Ella Fitzgerald with white dress sang "sofisticated lady".

Recipe:
- 4 cl gin
- 3 cl of triple sec or Cointreau
- 2 cl fresh lemon juice
- 1 lemon washer

Take a cocktail glass and fill it with ice to cool it. In a cocktail shaker filled with ice pour 4 cl gin 3 cl of triple sec and 2 cl fresh lemon juice.
Shake well and then strain into a cocktail glass emptied of ice. Garnish with a slice of lemon on the glass. Serve without straw.

Yellow bird

• Category: Drinks New Era.
• Glass: cocktail glass.

Some authors argue that this cocktail was designed to celebrate a record of the Mills Brothers, a vocal group jazz and American pop, born in 1928 and still active through his musical heirs. A now has more than 2,000 recordings, 50 million records sold and at least three dozen gold records. In 1998 he was admitted to the Vocal Group Hall of Fame.
Originally there were four African-American brothers, born in Piqua (Ohio): John Jr., low (voice) and guitar, Herbert, tenor, Harry, and baritone Donald Mills, tenor soloist.

Recipe:
- 3 cl White rum
- 1.5 cl Galliano
- 1.5 cl Triple Sec
- 1.5 cl of lime juice.

Pour the rum, Galliano liqueur, Triple Sec and juice (fresh and filtered) lime in a shaker with ice.
Shake well and strain into a cocktail glass previously cooled.
Garnish with a slice of lemon.

Other Cocktails

In addition to the list of 77 cocktails made official on Nov. 25, 2011 by IBA, there are a myriad of other cocktails that still deserve to be mentioned for both their previous membership in the above list, it is because they have been served in all the bars in the world; We mention, just as an example: Gibson, Czarina, Alaska, Grand Slam, Old pal, Gin and french, Bronx, etc..

Alaska

- Category: After Dinner Cocktail.
- Glass: cocktail glass.

Born in the United States at the beginning of the century, it is a classic cocktail, easy to prepare, good relaxing and good digestive.
Alaska cocktail is his first recording in a cookbook of 1913, in the book by Jacques Straub "Straub's manual of mixed drinks.", Which sees the presence of ingredients such as Orange Bitters, Yellow Chartreuse and Tom gin.
Subsequently appear in the cookbook Harry Craddock "The Savoy Cocktail Book" in which in addition to its coding, leaving us a little note.

Recipe:
- 3/4 of gin
- 1/4 Chartreuse yellow.

Prepare in a shaker with some ice cubes, pouring, in order, the Gin (preferably Dry Gin) and then the Chartreuse.
Serve in a well chilled cocktail glass.
There is a variant that adds a correction to traditional ingredients with a few drops of Bitter Orange.

Alpage

• Category: After Dinner Cocktail.
• Glass: Martini cup.

Recipe:
- 2cl white rum
- 1 cl Cointreau
- 1 cl Mandarinetto
- 1 cl sugar syrup
- 1 cl Espresso coffee
- 1 cl Cream milk surface.

Pour into a shaker with ice all the ingredients, except the milk cream. Pour the drink into a chilled martini and finish pouring the cream on the surface....

Andalusia

• Category: Pre-Dinner Cocktail.
• Glass: cocktail glass.

Cocktail Andalusia, is a drink with an intense flavor and is particularly suitable as an aperitif and as an excellent digestive. Strong is his smell, the nose is richly aromatic. It should be drunk chilled, quenches thirst and intoxicates at the right point.

Recipe:
- 2/4 of dry Sherry
- 1/4 Brandy Carlos Primero
- 1/4 of Amaretto di Saronno.

It is prepared in a mixing glass with ice cubes.
It is poured into a cocktail glass and eventually squeezes an orange peel on the surface.
Someone replaces the Amaretto with light rum.

Annalisa

• Category: Pre-Dinner Cocktail.
• Glass: double cocktail glass.

It can be drunk as an aperitif or as a good after dinner. Cocktails for women for its color, although not so light as it seems.
For those who enjoy a cocktail sour and not too dry this drink is really amazing.
It should be drunk absolutely ghiacciatissimo.

Recipe:
* 1/3 Gin
* 1/3 Dry Vermouth
* 1/3 Cointreau
* 2 tablespoons lemon juice
* A dash of grenadine.

It is prepared in a mixing glass with ice cubes. Pour all ingredients, stir and serve in double cocktail glass previously cooled.

Anonimo

• Category: Pre-Dinner Cocktail.
• Glass: flute.

A cocktail that lends itself well as an aperitif, very similar to the
Kir (very famous in France) but slightly alcoholic.
Easy to prepare requiring only the finest ingredients for a perfect
aperitif and delicious.

Recipe:
- 3/4 cup dry white wine
- A dash of Cointreau
- A dash of strawberry syrup.

Pour the chilled wine in the cup or glass in the preferred, add the
other two ingredients and mix lightly with the bar cocktail.
Garnish with a strawberry on the edge or berries of your choice,
you may also want a lemon zest made a twist.
You can also be prepared with Prosecco or Franciacorta.

Bamboo

- Category: Pre-Dinner Cocktail.
- Glass: cocktail glass.

It is said that the legend of the "Bamboo Cocktail" begins in 1889, when a man of German origin, Louis Eppinger moved to Japan to direct the Grand Hotel in Yokohama.
Here from their hands, in the absence of Italian Vermouth, an indispensable ingredient for preparing the Adonis Cocktail and difficult to find, it was replaced by the French Vermouth, thus giving rise to the drink known as "Bamboo" cocktails that in no time, received a huge success by European and American customers.

Recipe:
- 1/2 of dry sherry
- 1/2 of dry vermouth
- A drop of orange bitters
- 3/4 ice cubes.

Put ice first and then one by one the other ingredients in a mixing-glass, then schekerare everything well, with strong sweetness and then filtered to provide the cocktails in the cocktail cup, previously cooled properly.
Finally, complete the presentation of the cup of the Bamboo, with a slice of fruit to taste.

Bentley

- Category: Pre-Dinner Cocktail.
- Glass: cocktail glass or tumbler if not shaken.

This classic French aperitif was born in the early twenties in Normandy on the initiative of a barman who wanted to give the cocktail he invented the name of a luxury car, English Bentley, who then were standing outside the hottest clubs and elegant coast.
But it is mainly in the United Kingdom that the drink was more successful, then entering rightly, in 1961, in the group of fifty cocktail world coding IBA.
Eliminated, wrongly, in the subsequent international catalogs, continues today to be great demand as an aperitif to the ease of preparation and to its pleasant taste.

Recipe:
- 1/2 of Calvados
- 1/2 Vermouth Dubonnet.

Put some in a mixing glass with ice cubes and add the remaining ingredients. Stir with a spoon to handle and pour into the glass. The cocktail is ready. It can also be served as a digestif.
It has recently been revised and with the addition of two sprays of Creme de Cassis and a little of Soda Schweppes becomes a good long drink that can be served at any time, including aperitif.

Blue Lagoon

• Category: Pre-Dinner Cocktail.
• Glass: cocktail glass.

Born in the '50s in Britain, the Blue Lagoon entered immediately in the recipe IBA drafted in 1961, and was later confirmed in the next two, with a difference.
The preparation is simple and the lemon juice together with the taste of the bitter orange blue Curacao give a hint of citrus scents very refreshing.

Recipe:
  • 1/10 Blue Curacao
  • 3/10 of lemon juice
  • 6/10 of vodka.

Shake all ingredients quickly with the ice crystal and pour, filtering, in a cocktail glass.
Finally, decorate with lemon zest placed on the edge of the cup.

Bronx

- Category: Pre-Dinner Cocktail.
- Glass: cocktail glass.

The Bronx is one of the cocktails that have made the history of the mixed drink. The recipe consists of Gin, Dry Vermouth, Red Vermouth and orange juice, entered the category of cocktails encoded IBA and here he remained for many years until 2012. It was probably created during the era of the American Prohibition and had the its boom around the thirties.

There are many legends about the birth of this drink, including the most reliable is the one that sees it as a creature born of the barman Johnnie Solon Hotel Manhattan in New York, one of the best barman of the time, who mixed first gin, martini and orange juice and when they asked him what his name was that new cocktails replied "it is the Bronx," referring to the Bronx Zoo, saw that his clients always told him that after drinking his cocktail saw strange animals.

The Bronx cocktail is tasty and not too sweet, "fruity" taste, without being trivial or sticky.

Recipe:
- 4 cl gin
- 2 cl red vermouth
- 2 cl dry vermouth
- 2cl of orange juice.

It is prepared in a shaker with the addition of ice. It serves cocktails in the cup and has no seals.

For the success of the cocktail it is important to use a high quality Gin.

Bull Shot

• Category: Long Drink.
• Glass: highball.

The Bull Shot is a cocktail that was born recently in North America as a variant of the Bloody Mary.
The basic element is always the vodka and even condiments do not change (lemon juice, Tabasco and Worcestershire sauce) but the tomato juice is substituted by another typical ingredient: beef broth or consommé.
The resulting low-alcohol cocktails, drink during the cocktail, but taste very strong and particular.

Recipe:
- 30% of Vodka
- 60% of meat stock
- 10%) of Lemon juice
- Worcester (a pinch)
- Tabasco (a pinch)
- Salt (a pinch)
- pepper (a pinch).

Prepare in a shaker pouring vodka, beef broth and lemon juice. Season with Worcester Sauce, Tabasco, salt and pepper and serve in a glass high ball. In winter it can be served hot.
In the hot version is prepared directly in the tumbler, placing the ingredients before the stirrer and then the hot consommé, vodka, lemon juice, drops of Worcestershire sauce, Tabasco, salt and pepper.

Cardinale

• Category: After Dinner Cocktail.
• Glass: cocktail glass.

Apparently it invented it was nothing less than a cardinal.
It is said, in fact, that during his stay in Rome, a cardinal was usually attend the Excelsior Hotel in Via Veneto, where he was preparing a mixture, indicating the barman personally doses and methods; the latter subsequently made his own recipe, leaders by tasting by others: thus collected a huge success and, grateful to the cardinal, titled him the cocktail, calling precisely Cardinal.
Others think that the name is due to the color of the liquid obtained, for the fact that is very similar to that referred to in the chromatic scale as a red cardinal.

Recipe:
- 5 cl of gin
- 3 cl dry vermouth
- 2 cl of Bitter Campari.

It is prepared in a mixing glass, mixing with the stirrer the three ingredients together in the ice crystal. Pour, filtering, in the cocktail cup and garnish with the lemon zest, placed on the edge and in the liquid part.

Caruso

Category: After Dinner Cocktail.
Glass: cocktail glass.

The Caruso is a classic after dinner that, after entering in the 50 IBA cocktail World Cup in 1961, was unfairly eliminated from subsequent codification.
This short drink the US was created around 1920-1925 in honor of the great Neapolitan tenor Enrico Caruso. Ideal for lovers of mixtures rather strong and aromatic, can be eaten after dinner that throughout the evening.

Recipe:
- 1/3 of gin
- 1/3 of dry vermouth
- 1/3 of cream mint green

Put in a shaker Gin, Dry Vermouth and mint cream (green). Add the ice crystal and shake vigorously for a few seconds. Strain into a chilled cocktail.

Claridge

• Category: Pre-Dinner Cocktail.
• Glass: cocktail glass.

It is the classic pre dinner born in the early twentieth century and also has distinct characteristics of cocktails from the afternoon fades if the dose of vermouth.
Born in Britain at the beginning of the century, it took the name of a famous London hotel. Quoted in the first codification of IBA cocktail World 1961, it was then removed from subsequent. It is still cited in all the major international cookbooks and always finds admirers ready to appreciate the unmistakable scent.

Recipe:
- 1/3 of gin
- 1/3 of dry vermouth
- 1/6 Cointreau
- 1/6 of apricot brandy.

Put in a mixing glass clear ice and ingredients and, after mixing quickly, pour filtering with the strainer into the bowl cocktail.

Czarina

• Category: After Dinner Cocktail.
• Glass: cocktail glass.

It is one of the first American cocktail where the vodka is used after the end of World War II.
Originally scheduled as an aperitif strong (the basic recipe was to use vodka to 50 degrees), it has become with the passage of time to consume a cocktail in the evening and at night.
Including 50 in the World Cup cocktail in the codification of '61, it has not been confirmed in later. Although it is not required in recent times, it remains one of the "pillars" in the history of mixed drinks.

Recipe:
- 2/4 of vodka
- 1/4 of dry vermouth
- 1/4 of apricot brandy
- a drop of Angostura.

Place the ingredients in a mixing glass with ice crystal and, after mixing gently, pour filtering with the strainer into the bowl cocktail.

Gibson

• Category: Pre-Dinner Cocktail.
• Glass: cocktail glass.

It is nothing but a small change to the better known Cocktail Martini consists of an onion and sour, as well as an imbalance of proportions in favor of gin.
It is said that Gibson takes its name from Charles Dana Gibson, illustrator of "Life", which ordered the player's club in New York a special coktail Martini: the face of this request, the bartender replaced the olive green as decoration with a little onion in bittersweet, discovering the power of taste.
The bartenders have also taken steps to adjust the doses of liquor, reducing the vermouth and gin increasing, whose bitterness is surely kept at bay by the slightly sweet taste of the onion.

Recipe:
  • 6 cl gin
  • 1 cl Dry Vermouth.

Pour the gin and vermouth Dry in a mixing glass with ice, shake and servrlo in a well chilled cocktail glass.
Its seal is a sweet and sour onion.
The old recipe was expressed in tenths (9/10 Gin 1/10 dry vermouth).

Gin & French

• Category: Pre-Dinner Cocktail.
• Glass: cocktail glass or highball (if you add tonic water).

Gin and French was produced for the first time in the United States during the thirties. Originally called "fifty-fifty" because the doses of gin and vermouth used were the same, it was later modified by the introduction of French vermouth, decreasing the amount of gin and changing name.
This cocktail of traditional flavor is a great pre-dinner aperitif.

Recipe:
- 6/10 gin
- 4/10 of vemouth dry
- lemon zest.

Put a little ice in a mixing glass, add gin and vermouth, stir vigorously and strain into a cocktail glass. To complete rub lemon zest dl on the surface.
Remember not to use the lemon zest for decoration, the original version is without gasket.
Serving the cocktail in a highball glass filled with tonic water you get a good long drink after dinner.
One of the best brands of French vermouth Noilly-Prat is, that you can also find in Italy.

Gin & It

• Category: Pre-Dinner Cocktail.
• Glass: cocktail glass.

The cocktail Gin & It was born in the thirties as a variant of Italian Gin & French; In fact, in its composition, in addition to Gin, using the Italian red vermouth instead of the dry French and change the amount slightly (more Gin and Vermouth less).
Remains a cocktail drink much alcohol (about 27 °) but, being softened by red vermouth, it is sweeter and more aromatic gin and French.

Recipe:
• 4.9 cl Gin
• 2.1 cl Red Vermouth.

Put some ice cubes in a mixing glass and add the other ingredients. Stir for a few seconds with the bar spoon and pour into a cocktail glass previously cooled.
Garnish with a cocktail cherry.

Golden Cadillac

• Category: After Dinner Cocktail.
• Glass: cocktail glass.

The Golden cadillac is a cocktail belonging to the category of after dinner, made with Galliano liqueur and creme de cacao. Created in New York in the 50s and 60s American Roger's Bar in honor of the film "The Solid Gold Cadillac," is not very alcoholic cocktails creamy and sweet taste.
The presence of Galliano gives it a very spicy aroma, this is a drink after dinner, to accompany dessert or a drink together in the winter evenings.

Recipe:
  • 3 cl liqueur Galliano
  • 3 cl cream cocoa clear
  • 3 cl fresh cream.

Chill a bowl with 3 ice cubes. Mettetene other 4 in a shaker, add cream, Galliano liqueur and creme de cacao and agitated with panache.
Empty the cup and pour the drink, filtering with the strainer.
Garnish with a slice of orange to add a refreshing touch.

Grand Slam

• Glass: cocktail glass.

The drink in question appears for the first time in the manual of Harry Craddock 1930 "The Savoy Cocktail Book", the book that will take its name from the hotel in London.

Recipe:
- 5 cl Punch Swedish
- 2 cl Red Vermouth
- 2 cl Dry Vermouth.

Prepared directly in the shaker, shekerato with ice and then filtered into the glass.
Cool the glass and the boston shaker eliminating the water produced in the latter stage. Pour all ingredients, making sure that the ice is crystal clear; shekerare and filter with the strainer directly into the cup cocktail.

Jack Rose

• Category: After Dinner Cocktail.
• Glass: cocktail glass.

Numerous stories about its origin. The first version says that he was the inventor Frank May, an American bartender whose nickname was "Jack Rose".
Another version says that the Jack Rose Cocktail has been paid for the first time around 1910 by Jacob Rosenzweig, an American gangster from the nickname precisely Jack Rose.
The third, not the last, but the most significant is that the Jack Rose cocktail was invented around 1920/30 by the bartender of the Inn, Nelson Fastige, which would created for Lisa Laird ancestor of the Scottish distiller William Laird's father Applelack, distilled apple a little 'sweeter than Calvados and very famous in the United States in 800 years.

Recipe:
- 4 cl Calvados
- 2 cl lemon juice
- 1 cl grenadine syrup.

Pour all ingredients into mixing previously Glass filled with ice, shake vigorously and pour into the bowl cocktail filtering with the appropriate pass.
Decoration with lemon slice or peel.

Japanese Slipper

• Category: Pre-Dinner Cocktail.
• Glass: cocktail glass.

A great mix of soft and fruity flavors, ideal for spring and summer.
The Japanese Slipper is a cocktail young, newly invented (1984) by JP Bourguignon in Melbourne, Australia. He had an instant success and is now one of the most famous cocktails around the world.
The Japanese Slipper is a mix lightweight and low in alcohol, easily absorbed, suitable for every type of drinker.
He combines well with Japanese food, for an aperitif fresh, modern and light.

Recipe:
  • 3 cl Midori
  • 3 cl Cointreau (or more triple sec)
  • 3 cl lemon juice
  • 1 piece of melon
  • 1 cocktail cherry
  • Honey q.s.

Filled with ice up to half the shaker Boston (one with a piece of glass), pour the Midori, Cointreau and lemon juice. Shake slowly in a circular motion.
Pour filtering with the strainer in the double cup cocktail.
To garnish frost with the piece of melon and honey infilzatelo then with a toothpick along with a cocktail cherry.

Ladyboy

• Category: After Dinner Cocktail.
• Glass: tumbler.

This cocktail was created by a press photographer, Phil Coburn who works for the London office of the Sunday Mirror. One night in 2003, Phil and his colleagues were in a hotel room in Jordan are ready to go to Iraq.
To alleviate boredom, Phil invented this cocktail (defined by him "terrible"), convincing even the barman at the Hotel Intercontinental in Amman it was a real cocktail.

Recipe:
* 3.5 cl Baileys Irish Cream
* 3.5 cl Brandy.

It is prepared by pouring baileys and brandy in a tumbler (old fashioned) with ice, stirring gently.
Finally garnish with a cinnamon stick and sprinkle with grated nutmeg.

Old Pal

• Category: Pre-Dinner Cocktail.
• Glass: cocktail glass.

Born in the United States in the 50s, this pre dinner became part of the first encoding IBA in 1961, with the use of the mixing glass and cup cocktail.
Today in America is consumed mainly in the variant On the Opening Cocktail, and indicates a drink completely different from that proposed in the card and consists of: 1/2 oz. grenadine, 1/2 ounce of red vermouth, 1 and 1/2 oz blended whiskey.
It was prepared in a mixing glass and cocktails served in the cup and it was recommended for consumption afternoon, evening and night. Despite the Old Pal no longer been part of the next World IBA recipe, it remains a classic in the history of mixing and is indicated as excellent sundowners.

Recipe:
  • 1/3 of Rye whiskey
  • 1/3 of dry vermouth
  • 1/3 of bitter Campari.

Place them all ingredients in a mixing glass with ice and stir in gently.
The preparation must then poured into a chilled martini type of eliminating the ice.

Orgasm

• Category: After Dinner Cocktail.
• Glass: tumbler.

The Orgasm is a very popular cocktail that the bartender interpreted in the most imaginative ways possible depending on personal taste.
It is a cocktail strong flavor and creamy texture that gives characteristics similar to those of a shot: usually drink in one breath, but can also be sipped after dinner enjoying the full flavor of the mixture.

Recipe:
* 3 cl Cointreau
* 3 cl Baileys Irish Cream
* 2 cl Grand Marnier.

Pour ingredients directly in a glass like old fashioned, or in a shot glass, and garnish with a cocktail cherry.

Rob Roy

• Category: Pre-Dinner Cocktail.
• Glass: cocktail glass.

The Rob Roy is a cocktail pre dinner from reddish color and strong flavor. It was invented in the late nineteenth century, as a bartender in New York for the first show of the homonymous opera.
Legend has it, however, it was created in Scotland by the manufacturers of whiskey, to honor the bandit and revolutionary hero Scottish Robert MacGregor, nicknamed Rob Roy for her red hair. This curious character became famous through the novel by Walter Scott.

Recipe:
- 4.5 cl Scotch whiskey
- 2.5 cl Sweet Vermouth
- 1 drop of angostura bitters.

Put some ice cubes in a mixing glass and let cool with gentle circular motions. Drain excess liquid.
Put the whiskey, vermouth and two drops of Angostura.
Mix everything with a long spoon. Pour into a cocktail glass, trying not to drop the remaining ice, and garnish with a cherry.

White Russian

• Category: After Dinner Cocktail.
• Glass: tumbler.

The White Russian is a cocktail made of vodka variant of the Black Russian.
Despite the significant alcohol content, it has a very delicate flavor and sweet, so it can be served as a "dessert".
The name translated means white Russian, refers both to the white color of the drink is the presence of the typical Russian vodka and also playing on the meaning of words, the deployment of the White (anti-Bolshevik) in the Russian civil war.

Recipe:
- 5.0 cl of vodka
- 2.0 cl coffee liqueur
- Cream.

It is preferable to use the Kahlua or failing that the Borghetti (its counterpart Italian), which however is not shown in the more bitter.
It prepares directly into old fashioned glass filled with ice. Pour vodka and liqueur into the glass and stir.
Subsequently pour the cream just mounted with the traditional shaker into the glass preferably by dropping it on an ice cube (or you can use the back of the spoon bar spoon).
It should not be adding any decoration and not be mixed.
It should also be served with a short-tube, in such a way that it can be slowly sip and mix.

Made in the USA
Monee, IL
07 July 2026